First World War
and Army of Occupation
War Diary
France, Belgium and Germany

25 DIVISION
7 Infantry Brigade
Manchester Regiment
20th Battalion
29 November 1916 - 30 June 1919

WO95/2244/4

The Naval & Military Press Ltd
www.nmarchive.com
Published in association with The National Archives

Published by

The Naval & Military Press Ltd

Unit 10 Ridgewood Industrial Park,

Uckfield, East Sussex,

TN22 5QE England

Tel: +44 (0) 1825 749494

www.naval-military-press.com

www.nmarchive.com

This diary has been reprinted in facsimile from the original. Any imperfections are inevitably reproduced and the quality may fall short of modern type and cartographic standards.

© Crown Copyright
Images reproduced by permission of The National Archives, London, England, 2015.

Contents

Document type	Place/Title	Date From	Date To
Heading	WO95/2244/4		
Heading	25th Division 7th Infy Bde 20th Bn Manchester Regt Sep 1918-Jun 1919 From Italy 7 Div. 23rd		
Heading	War Diary of 20th Battn The Manchester Regiment From 1st September 1918 To 30th September 1918. Vol 35		
War Diary	Italy Brogliano	01/09/1918	12/09/1918
War Diary	Italy	12/09/1918	14/09/1918
War Diary	Italy	13/09/1918	17/09/1918
War Diary	Italy France	13/09/1918	17/09/1918
War Diary	Sheet 14 Abbeville 1/100,000 K.5.	18/09/1918	27/09/1918
War Diary	Sheet 17 Amiens 1/100,000 G.1	28/09/1918	28/09/1918
Miscellaneous	20th Bn The Manchester Regiment. Appendix I	05/09/1918	05/09/1918
Miscellaneous	20th Bn. The Manchester Regiment. Order No. 147 Appendix III	11/09/1918	11/09/1918
Miscellaneous	20th Bn. The Manchester Regiment. Move Table to accompany Order No. 147	11/09/1918	11/09/1918
Operation(al) Order(s)	20th Bn. The Manchester Regiment. Addendum to Battalion Order No. 147 Appendix III	12/09/1918	12/09/1918
Miscellaneous	20th Bn. The Manchester Regiment. Appendix IV	20/09/1918	20/09/1918
Heading	War Diary of 20th Battn The Manchester Regt. From 1st October 1918 to 31st October 1918 Volume 36		
War Diary	France	01/10/1918	05/10/1918
War Diary	Map Ref Montbrehain	06/10/1918	08/10/1918
War Diary	France	09/10/1918	11/10/1918
War Diary	France Elincourt	12/10/1918	17/10/1918
War Diary	Marois	18/10/1918	18/10/1918
War Diary	St Benin	19/10/1918	19/10/1918
War Diary	In The Line S.E. Alechtehu	20/10/1918	20/10/1918
War Diary	Pommereuil	24/10/1918	24/10/1918
War Diary	Fontaine Au Bois	25/10/1918	26/10/1918
War Diary	In Reserve	27/10/1918	27/10/1918
War Diary	In Reserve	28/10/1918	30/10/1918
Miscellaneous	20th Bn. The Manchester Regiment. Appendix I	14/10/1918	14/10/1918
Miscellaneous	20th Battalion The Manchester Regiment. Appendix II	01/11/1918	01/11/1918
Miscellaneous	20th Battalion The Manchester Regiment. Nominal Roll Of Officers as on 31-10-18	31/10/1918	31/10/1918
Miscellaneous	20th Bn. The Manchester Regiment. Casualties During The Month Of October 1918	01/11/1918	01/11/1918
Heading	War Diary of 20th Battn The Manchester Regiment From 1st November 1918 To 30th November 1918 Volume 37		
War Diary	France	01/11/1918	03/11/1918
War Diary	Meap Forest 1/10,000	03/11/1918	04/11/1918
War Diary	France	04/11/1918	04/11/1918
War Diary	Map Sheet 57A 1/40,000	05/11/1918	06/11/1918
War Diary	France	06/11/1918	06/11/1918
War Diary	Map Sheet 57A 1/40,000	06/11/1918	06/11/1918
War Diary	France	06/11/1918	06/11/1918
War Diary	Map Sheet 57A 1/40,000	06/11/1918	06/11/1918

War Diary	France	06/11/1918	06/11/1918
War Diary	Map Sheet 57A 1/40,000	06/11/1918	07/11/1918
War Diary	France	07/11/1918	07/11/1918
War Diary	Sheet 57A 1/40000	08/11/1918	11/11/1918
War Diary	France Sheet 57 A 1/40,000	11/11/1918	17/11/1918
War Diary	Pommereuil	18/11/1918	20/11/1918
War Diary	Sheet 57A 1/40,000	21/11/1918	26/11/1918
War Diary	Pommereuil Sheet 57A 1/40,000	27/11/1918	28/11/1918
War Diary	Map Valenciennes 1/100,000	29/11/1916	30/11/1916
Miscellaneous	20th Bn. The Manchester Regiment. Order No. 153 Appendix I	02/11/1918	02/11/1918
Miscellaneous	20th Bn. The Manchester Regiment. Appendix II	03/11/1918	03/11/1918
Miscellaneous	20th Bn. The Manchester Regiment. Appendix III		
Miscellaneous	20th Manchester Regiment Appendix IV	13/11/1918	13/11/1918
Miscellaneous	20th Bn. The Manchester Regiment Order No. 155. Appendix V	29/11/1918	29/11/1918
Miscellaneous	20th Battalion The Manchester Regiment.	01/12/1918	01/12/1918
Miscellaneous	20th Bn. The Manchester Regiment.	01/12/1918	01/12/1918
Miscellaneous	20th Battalion the Manchester Regiment.	01/12/1918	01/12/1918
Heading	War Diary of 20th Battalion The Manchester Regiment From 1st December 1918 To 31st December 1918 Volume XXXVIII		
War Diary	Quievy Sheet 57B 1/40,000	01/12/1918	09/12/1918
War Diary	Fontaine Au Pire	10/12/1918	16/12/1918
War Diary Map	Fontaine Au Pire Sheet 57B 1/40000	17/12/1918	31/12/1918
Operation(al) Order(s)	20th Bn. The Manchester Regiment. Order No. 156	08/12/1918	08/12/1918
Operation(al) Order(s)	20th Bn. The Manchester Regiment. Order No. 157	31/12/1918	31/12/1918
Miscellaneous	20th Bn. The Manchester Regiment.	03/01/1919	03/01/1919
Heading	War Diary of 20th Battalion The Manchester Regiment From 1st January, 1919. To, 31st January 1919 Volume XXXIX		
War Diary	France Valenciennes	01/01/1919	01/01/1919
War Diary	Briastre	02/01/1919	03/01/1919
War Diary	Poix Du Nord Sheet 57b 1/40,000	04/01/1919	12/01/1919
War Diary	Poix Du Nord	13/01/1919	31/01/1919
Operation(al) Order(s)	20th Bn. The Manchester Regiment. Order No. 158	02/01/1919	02/01/1919
Miscellaneous	20th Battalion The Manchester Regiment.	03/02/1919	03/02/1919
Heading	War Diary of 20th Battalion The Manchester Regiment From, 1st February, 1919 To, 28th February 1919 Volume XL		
War Diary	Poix Du Nord	01/02/1919	02/02/1919
War Diary	Sheet 57B 1/40,000	03/02/1919	16/02/1919
War Diary	Poix Du Nord	17/02/1919	18/02/1919
War Diary	Sheet 57B 1/40000	19/02/1919	19/02/1919
War Diary	St Vaast	20/02/1919	20/02/1919
War Diary	Cambrai	21/02/1919	26/02/1919
War Diary	Cambrai Sheet 57B 1/40,000	28/02/1919	28/02/1919
Operation(al) Order(s)	20th Bn. The Manchester Regiment. Order No. 159	18/02/1919	18/02/1919
Miscellaneous	20th Bn. The Manchester Regiment.	02/03/1919	02/03/1919
Miscellaneous	20th Bn. The Manchester Regiment.		
Heading	War Diary of 20th Battalion The Manchester Regiment From, 1st March 1919 To 31st March 1919 Volume XLI		
War Diary	Cambrai	01/03/1919	31/03/1919
Miscellaneous	20th Bn. The Manchester Regiment.	31/03/1919	31/03/1919

Heading	War Diary of 2nd Battalion The Manchester Regiment. 1st April to 30th April 1919 Volume XXXXII		
War Diary	Cambrai	01/04/1919	30/04/1919
Miscellaneous	20th Bn. The Manchester Regiment.	02/05/1919	02/05/1919
War Diary	Cambrai	01/05/1919	30/06/1919

WO 95/22441

25TH DIVISION
7TH INFY BDE

20TH BN MANCHESTER REGT
SEP 1918 – JUN 1919

from ITALY 7 DIV. 22 Bde

Secret.

[Stamp: 20th BATTALION, THE MANCHESTER REGIMENT. No......... Date.........]

War Diary

— of —

20th Battn. The Manchester Regiment.

— From 1st September, 1918 To 30th September, 1918 —

Volume 35.

G.B. Dumpsey
Capt. & Adjutant
for Lieut. Colonel.

Commdg. 20th Battn The Manchester Regiment

Sep '18
to
June '19

Sheet 1.

WAR DIARY
or
INTELLIGENCE SUMMARY.

(Erase heading not required.)

VOLUME XXXV. SEPTEMBER 1918.

Army Form C. 2118.

Place	Date	Hour	Summary of Events and Information	Remarks and references to Appendices
ITALY BROGLIANO	1st		Church Parade in the morning. Weather fine and sunny.	T.M.L
"	2nd		No parades in the morning, a wet day.	T.M.L
"	3rd		Musketry Shots at TRISSINO. The whole battalion marched to the ground and spent the day there. Weather fine and bright.	T.M.L
"	4th–7th		Training as per programme. Classification of battalion in musketry practices on 4th 5th and 6th. Battalion scheme on 7th. Weather fine and bright.	T.M.L
"	8th–11th		Training according to programme. Weather a thunderstorm on the evening of 8th made a break in the spell of fine weather 9th–11th Dull and overcast, much cooler. On the 11th news of move to France received. Drill uniforms and sunshades handed in and Service Dress drawn.	APPENDIX I
"	12th		Preparation for entrainment at 8.45 a.m. Battalion paraded for address by the Divisional Commander who thanked the officers N.C.Os and men for the good work done by the battalion while in the 7th Division	T.M.L

Sheet 2.

Army Form C. 2118.

WAR DIARY
INTELLIGENCE SUMMARY.

VOLUME XXXV (Cont.) SEPTEMBER 1918.

Place	Date	Hour	Summary of Events and Information	Remarks and references to Appendices
ITALY	12th (Cont.)		and much regretted the Battalion leaving the Division. Italian decorations for good work in connection with the last push done by the Battalion were presented by the Divisional Commander to the commanding officer (Lieut Col. BURT. D.S.O) Lieut SHACKLE M.C M.M. WILLIAMS and P.te HORTON D.C.M.	T.M.K.
"	13th		In the early hours of the morning the personnel of the 1st train left for embussment at 3.36 a.m. On main CORNEDO - MONTECCHIO Road East of BROGLIANO, entraining at VICENZA for France.	T.M.K.
"	14th		Remainder of Battalion embussed same hour and place as above.	
	13th-17th		The Commanding Officer (Lt. Col. C.S. BURT. D.S.O) Adjt. M.O. T.O. Q.M. & H.Q. Coy. A and B Coys. entrained at VICENZA on the 13th. Train left at 7.36 a.m. On the 14th at the same hour and place 2 H.Q. Coy, C. & D. Coys under command of 2nd in Command entrained. Route for both trains. VICENZA, VERONA, BRESCIA, outskirts of MILAN, TURIN, Mt CENIS Tunnel to MODANE, MONTMELIAN, AIX-LES-BAINS, LES LAUMES, MONTEREAU, VILLENEUVE outskirts of PARIS, AMIENS and ABBEVILLE, 1st half Battalion detrained at PONT REMY arriving on 16th	APPENDICES II & III T.M.K.

Sheet. 3

Army Form C. 2118.

WAR DIARY
or
INTELLIGENCE SUMMARY.
(Erase heading not required.)

VOLUME XXXV (Cont'd)   SEPTEMBER 1918.

Place	Date	Hour	Summary of Events and Information	Remarks and references to Appendices
ITALY — FRANCE.	13-17th		(Cont'd.) and marched to billets at DRUCAT (via VAUCHELLES Les QUESNOY) 2nd Half Battalion detrained at ST RIQUIER at 5.30 a.m. on 17th and marched to billets at CAOURS and DRUCAT. This battalion with 21st Manchester Regt and 9th/12th Devon Regt formed the 7th Brigade 25th Division H.Q. A & B. Coys in billets at DRUCAT. C and D Coys in billets at CAOURS. Billets on the whole quite good.	T.M.R.
Sheet 14 ABBEVILLE 100,000 K.5.	18th-26th		Reorganisation of the Battalion. Individual and Collective training carried out. On 26th Brigade Outpost Scheme. Weather unsettled. Rain fell on most days at intervals.	APPENDIX IV T.M.R.
	27th		Battalion (less 1st Transport) left at 3.40 p.m. for entrainment at ST. RIQUIER. 1st Transport entrained at PONT REMY, the other ½ left on the 25th by road. Battalion detrained at ALBERT at 1 a.m.	T.M.R.
Sheet 17 AMIENS. 100,000 9.1	28th		MILLENCOURT and HENENCOURT to billets at BAIZIEUX. Billets were poor and in a filthy condition. Transport rejoined battalion. Weather still showery.	T.M.R.

War Diary

APPENDIX I.

20th Bn The Manchester Regiment.

PROGRAMME OF TRAINING FOR WEEK-ENDING 15th SEPTEMBER. 1918.

Date.	Time.	Training.	Coy.	Place.
9th Sept. Monday.	7.0 to 10.30 a.m.	Musketry Practices.	A.	Battn. Range
		Coys in Attack Practices Up-hill, through woods etc., in various formations.	B. C. D.	AGNO Valley & M.GREGA.
Tuesday. 10th Sept.	7.0 a.m. to 10.30 a.m.	Musketry Practices.	B.	Battn. Range
		As Yesterday.	A. C. D.	AGNO Valley & M.GREGA.
Wednesday. 11th Sept.	7.0 a.m. to 10.30 a.m.	Musketry Practices.	C.	Battn. Range
		As Yesterday.	A. B. D.	AGNO Valley & M.GREGA.
Thursday. 12th Sept.	7.0 a.m. to 10.30 a.m.	Musketry Practices.	D.	Battn. Range
		As Yesterday.	A. B. C.	AGNO Valley & M.GREGA.
Friday. Sept.13th.	5.0 a.m. to 12.noon.	Battalion Scheme, Forming up in dark preliminary to daybreak attack, pursuit of enemy, & establishment of Outpost line.	All Coys	AGNO Valley & Hills to E M.GREGA.
Saturday. 14th Sept.	7.0 a.m. to 10.30 a.m.	Field Firing and Up-Hill attack.	All Coys.	CANTONE Range & Area.
Sunday. 15th Sept.		Baths & Recreation.		

NOTES - 5.0 p.m. to 6.30 p.m. daily. Lewis Gun and Signal Classes, Instruction of third Class shots on Battalion Range. Reconnaissance by Officers and Senior N.C.Os for following days work, and Night Compass marching.

G B Dempsey

Lieut.Colonel,
Cdg. 20th Bn. THE MANCHESTER REGIMENT.

5.9.18.

S E C R E T.   *War diary*   Copy No. III

10th BN. THE MANCHESTER REGIMENT.
ORDER No. 147.

APPENDIX II

1. The Battalion will move according to the attached Table on the 12th and 13th September, entraining at VICENZA.
2. Troops will arrive at the entraining Station 1 hour, and Transport with the necessary loading parties 3 hours, before the advertised time of departure of the train.
3. Trains will be comprised as under :-
   - Coaches — 3. 1st Class.
   - Covered Vans. 25.
   - Flats. 11.
   - Brake Vans. 2.
   - —
   - 40.

4. The first train conveying half H.Q., Half Transport, 'A' and 'B' Coys leaves VICENZA at 4.56 a.m. on the 13th instant. The second train, conveying half H.Q., half Transport, 'C' and 'D' Coys leaves VICENZA at 22.16 hours (10.16 p.m.) on the 13th instant.
5. The Battalion will be conveyed to VICENZA by lorry. The Transport will proceed by March route along main road followed by Tramway through MONTECCHIO to VICENZA. The Battalion will entrain in Service Dress - Full Marching Order. Rations for the day of entrainment to be carried on the man.
6. The A.D.M.S. is issuing instructions regarding the Medical arrangements for the journey.
7. Trucks for forage and rations will be located in the centre of the train as far as possible.
8. The E.F.C. is arranging a Canteen to be at the Station.
9. RATIONS. (a) 8 days rations and fuel for cooking, and 8 days forage for animals, as shown in Appendix "A" will be put on the train, in addition to the rations for the day of entrainment, which will be carried on the man.
   (b) The supply portion of the Divisional Train will be entrained loaded with one days rations for use the day following the day of detrainment. These rations are included in those referred to in para (a) above.
   (c) Arrangements are being made if possible for bread to be issued en route at ST.GERMAIN AU MONT D'OR. If this is possible further instructions will be issued later.
   In any case, full biscuit rations will be loaded on entrainment and returned later if not required.
10. One new blanket per man will be conveyed to the Station by Motor lorry.
11. HORSES.
(a) Whenever possible, accommodation for saddlery and gear should be found in the trucks, other than those used by the horses.
(b) Not more than six H.D. horses should be put in one truck. Higher trucks should be reserved for M.D. Horses.
(c) No Oats will be fed for the first 12 hours after entrainment.
(d) Hay nets and water buckets will be taken up to the full scale allowed.
(e) Tails will be bandaged whenever possible before entrainment and care will be taken that horses are not tied too far back in the trucks.
(f) If possible ashes or sand should be placed in the truck to give foot-hold. This must be arranged by Units at the entraining Station.
(g) Units to be complete with one Horse-rug, but these rugs only to be used on clipped horses.
(h) Ventilation of trucks is most important and should be regulated according to whether the truck is in motion or halted. Pneumonia was caused on the move from France to Italy in several cases by insufficient ventilation having been given during the journey.
(i) The door on the side of the running way must be kept closed.
(j) Personnel of A.V.C. should be distributed between trains to the best advantage.
(k) Galvanised pails, petrol tins or paraffin tins, up to a capacity of 24 gallons per truck, will be supplied for carrying water. These will be provided at entraining railheads under Divisional arrangements.
(l) Water will be available at each Halte Repas.
(m) Cooking and fires of any description are forbidden in Horse Trucks.
(n) Horses will be entrained by their own drivers, and not by the Fatigue party.
(o) Great care must be taken to see that horses are securely roped in the trucks, as during previous movements of troops, accidents occurred owing to lack of this precaution. All the ropes required are to be provided by the Unit.

12. (a) Men are forbidden to travel on the tops of the trucks.
(b) No one will be permitted to get out of the train until the bugle sounds "Dismiss". On the call "Fall in" being sounded, all ranks will at once enter the trucks.
(c) Os.C.'A' and 'B'Coys will detail Orderly Officers and Guards who will take tours of duty on the fore and rear portions of the first train. Os.C. 'C' and 'D'Coys will detail similar Orderly Officers and Guards for the second train. The duties of the Orderly Officers will be :-
  (i) To be on duty at each halt.
  (ii) To see to the issue of rations and meals.
  (iii) To enforce the rules detailed in para.(a) and (b) above.
(d) The Guards will be posted on the Track at each halt, in front of the engine, and behind the rear truck, to see that no one leaves the train without authority, nor leaves the precincts of the Station at Haltes Repas.
Orderly Officers will remain with that portion of the train for which they are detailed during the whole of their tours of duty.
(e) In each truck and compartment there will be a Senior N.C.O. detailed who will be responsible for the carrying out of the above orders.

13. SANITARY ARRANGEMENTS. Os.C.Coys will each detail Sanitary parties of one N.C.O. and four men. Each train will be provided with :
  2 Spades   4 Brooms.
  2 Shovels   20 Sandbags (if obtainable)
  1 Drum Chloride of Lime.

At Halts where military latrines are not provided, Sanitary squads will dig trench latrines which will be filled in before departure. At fixed halts all carriages and trucks will be swept out by Sanitary squads. Disinfectant is only to be used in emergencies and will not be used for sweeping up dirt.
Spitting in vehicles is to be made a subject of disciplinary action.

                    (Sgd) G.B.DEMPSEY,
11th Sept, 1918.   Captain & Adjutant.

20th Bn. THE LANCHESTER REGIMENT.

MOVE TABLE to accompany ORDER No.147.

Serial.	Date.	No. of 3 ton lorries.	Time.	Convey to.	Remarks.
1.	12th.	1.	Bn.H.Q. 10.0 a.m.	VICENZA.	R.Q.M.S. & 12 O.R. to unload Rations lorries & take charge of rations until entrainment.
2.	12th.	4.	Bn.H.Q. 4.30 p.m.	VICENZA.	For Stores & Blankets. To be loaded overnight. These lorries will remain with & be at disposal of the Battalion until completion of entrainment.
3.	12.	3.	Bn.H.Q. 7.30 p.m.	VICENZA.	Convey loading party of 1 Officer & 50 O.R. of 'C'Coy. These will take full kit & rations for day of entrainment & report to Entraining Officer, VICENZA.

An Advance party of Coy Clerks under Lt.LEES will proceed by these 3 lorries under Serial 3. to mark off carriages & coaches for both trains and hand to entraining Officer duplicate Entraining States for each train

4.	13th.	20.	Head of column at Cross Roads on main CORNEDO-MONTECCHIO Road at Point 159 about 1 kilo.m. due East of BROGLIANO facing South at 1.0 a.m.	Convey half the Battalion.
5.	13th.	20.	do. do. 4.0 p.m.	Do.

All Train kits and Mess Kits will be dumped at the Q.M.Stores by 9.0 p.m. on the 12th for the first train and by 2.0 p.m. on the 13th for the second train.   The Q.M. will arrange the journeys of the lorries accordingly.   Dixies will be carried on the Cooker.
Officer's large kits will be dumped at the Q.M.Stores at 7.0 p.m. 12th for first train.
Officers large kits will be dumped at the Q.M.Stores at 12.0 noon, 13th for second train.

The Transport Officer will despatch the two halves of the Transport so as to arrive at the Entraining Station three hours before the departure of the trains. -
        Approximate times 8.50 p.m. on the 12th.
                              2.0 p.m. on the 13th.
The Signal Officer will obtain the correct time and circulate it to all concerned at noon on the 12th.inst.

Lorry Allotment.
    Serial 4.   Half H.Q. - 4 lorries.
                    'A'Coy.   8   "
                    'B' ..   8   "

    Serial 5.   Half H.Q. - 4 lorries.
                    'C'Coy. - 8   "
                    'D' .. - 8   "

An Officer or Senior N.C.O. will be in charge of each lorry. Companies will be drawn up on the right of the road alongside their lorries allotted by the times detailed in Serials 4 & 5.

                                                         (Sgd) G.B.DEMPSEY,
11th Sept, 1918.   Captain & Adjutant.

20th Bn. THE MANCHESTER REGIMENT.

APPENDIX III

ADDENDUM to Battalion Order No.147.

Cancel the Lorry Table and times of trains issued under B.O.147 and substitute the following :- 1st Train 7.30 a.m. 13th inst: 2nd Train 7.30 a.m. 14th inst. (The remainder of the Orders hold good.)

Serial No.	Date.	No. of 3 ton Lorries.	Report.	Time.	Convey to.	Remarks.
1.	12th.	3.	Bn.H.Q.	7.p.m.	VICENZA.	Loading Party of 1 Officer & 50 O.R. from 'B'Coy. To take full kits and rations for the 13th inst., Load & travel by 1st train.

An Advance Party of Coy Clerks under Lt.LEES will proceed by these three lorries under Serial No.1. to mark carriages and hand in entraining States.

2.	12th.	3.	Bn.H.Q.	7.p.m.	VICENZA.	Baggage & Stores.
3.	13th.	20.	Head of column at Cross Rds on main CORMEDO-MONTECCHIO Rd at point 159.	3.36 a.m.	do.	Convey half H.Q. 'A' & 'B'Coys.
4.	13th.	3.	Bn.H.Q.	7.p.m.	do.	Loading Party of 1 Officer & 50 O.R. from 'C'Coy To take full kits & rations for 14th inst. Load & travel by 2nd train.
5.	13th.	3.	Bn.H.Q.	7.p.m.	do.	Baggage & Stores.
6.	14th.	20.	Head of Column at Cross Rds on main CORMEDO - MONTECCHIO Rd at point 159.	3.36 a.m.	do.	Convey Half H.Q. 'C' & 'D'Coys.

Lorries will remain with Battalion until Move is complete.

(a) Men will march with Steel Helmets on the packs under the straps of the packs. Blankets will be carried rolled on the top of the packs.

(b) All train kits and Mess Kits will be dumped at Q.M. Stores by 7.0 p.m. on the 12th for the first train and by 7.p.m. on the 13th for the second train. The Q.M. will arrange lorry journeys accordingly. Dixies to be carried on Cookers. Officers large Kits will be dumped at the Q.M.Stores at 9.30 p.m. 12th inst., for first train and at 9.30 p.m. 13th inst., for second train.

(c) Lorry Allotment.
    Serial 3. Half H.Q.   4 Lorries.
               'A'Coy.   8 "
               'B' ..   8 "

    Serial 6. Half H.Q.   4 Lorries.
               'C'Coy.   8 "
               'D' ..   8 "

(d) An Officer or Senior N.C.O. will be inc charge of each lorry. Companies will be drawn up on the right of the road alongside their lorries allotted, by the times detailed in Serials 3 & 6.

(e) The T.O. will despatch the two halves of the Transport so as to arrive at the Entraining Station 3 hours before the departure of the Train.
    Approximate Times.   11.30 p.m.   12th Sept.
    of Departure from   11.30 p.m.   13th Sept.
    BROGLIANO.

(f) The doors on the running side of the train will be kept closed except at halts.

x Ref details of entraining :- 1st Train - to list of vehicles add one S.A.A. Limber: to list of animals add 2 L.D

12.9.18.
                                   (Sgd) G.B.DEMPSEY,
                                   Captain & Adjutant.

20th Bn. THE MANCHESTER REGIMENT.   APPENDIX IV

PROGRAMME OF TRAINING FOR WEEK ENDING Friday 27th Sept. 1918.

Date.	Time.	Training.
Saturday. 21st Sept.	9.0 to 10.0 a.m.	Practise passing Messages. Rapid Loading & Aiming, as per G.181/9 of Aug.14
	10.0 to 11.0 a.m.	**Fire orders & fire direction and control.** Description of Targets.
	11.0 to 12.noon.	Platoons advancing in Artillery formation and thence into extended order.
Monday. Sept. 23rd.	9.0 to 10.0 a.m.	As above.
	10.0 a.m. to 12.noon.	Rapid deploy from Column of Route into platoons in Artillery formation, thence into sections, and finally into extended order.
	2.0 to 4.0 p.m.	Testing Classes for Lewis Gunners, Bombers, and Signallers. Tactical handling of Lewis Gun. Instruction in Bombing and use of Rifle Grenades for Rifle sections. 'A' Coy Lewis Gunners on 40 yards Range.
Tuesday. Sept. 24th.	9.0 to 10.0 a.m.	Gas Instruction.
	10.0 to 12.noon.	Platoons in attack on Strong Point. Great attention must be paid to covering fire.
	2.0 to 4.0 p.m.	As for Monday. 'B' Coy Lewis Gunners on 40 yards Range.
Wednesday. Sept. 25th.	9.0 to 10.0 a.m.	As for Monday.
	10 to 12.	Coys in Attack. Fire and movement.
	2 to 4 p.m.	As for Monday. 'C' Coy Lewis Gunners on 40 yards Range.
Thursday. Sept. 26th.	9.0 a.m. to 12.0 noon.	Battalion in Attack.
	2.to 4.p.m.	As for Monday. 'D' Coy Lewis Gunners on 40 yards Range.
Friday. Sept. 27th.	9.0 a.m. to 12.noon.	Battalion advancing in Battle formation. and Changing direction.
	2.to 4.p.m.	As for Monday. 'A' Coy Lewis Gunners on 40 yards Range.

All the above training will take place in the Battalion area.
Coys must notify Orderly Room, the day before, where they are going to carry out their next days training.
In all attacks particular attention must be paid to Fire Orders and Fire movement.

B Dempsey Capt/Major,
Cdg.20th Bn. THE MANCHESTER REGIMENT.

20.9.18.

SECRET.

ORIGINAL

7/25

20th BATTALION,
THE MANCHESTER
REGIMENT
No. 648
Date. 2/11/18

Vol 36

War Diary

—— of ——

20th Batt<u>n</u> The Manchester Regt.

from 1st October 1918 To 31st October 1918

Volume 36

C R Pilkington Lieut. Colonel.
Commdg 20th Bn. The Manchester Regt.

Army Form C. 2118.

WAR DIARY
or
INTELLIGENCE SUMMARY.

(Erase heading not required.)

VOLUME XXVI   OCTOBER 1918.

Instructions regarding War Diaries and Intelligence Summaries are contained in F. S. Regs, Part II. and the Staff Manual respectively. Title pages will be prepared in manuscript.

Place	Date	Hour	Summary of Events and Information	Remarks and references to Appendices
FRANCE	1st		Battalion marched via GUILLEMONT, COMBLES, BOUCHAVESNES, MOISLAINS to Bois de l'EPINETTE. Camp had to be pitched on arrival of tent and bivouacs.	T.M.K.
	2nd		Battalion pitched the attack in the morning. Individual training in the afternoon. Sudden orders received at 4.40 p.m. to move at 5.17 p.m. Marched via LIERAMONT VILLERS-FAUCON, St EMILIE to field on St EMILIE – RONSSOY Road near Bois de RONSSOY. Arrived about 8.15 p.m. No camp there but bivouacs arrived about 10 p.m. March. Fine morning and afternoon, but slight rain during whole of march.	T.M.K.
	3rd		Battalion moved occasionally during early movements on QUERRIEMONT FARM HARGICOURT – BELLICOURT – MAUROY – ESTRÉES into line opposite BEAUREVOIR + PONCHAUX, relieving AUSTRALIANS. Relief completed about 1 A.M. 4.10.18. Night fine.	ff
	4th		In conjunction with 9th Bde Recon Regt the Battn attacked BEAUREVOIR + PONCHAUX. Got into back villages but could not hold on. Reasons B Officers 92 O.R. Lt BURT D.S.O. 2nd Lt FORSYTH, 2nd Lt WILKINSON, 2/Lt POULTON, 2/Lt SEDDON	Oppendie I

SHEET 2

WAR DIARY
or
INTELLIGENCE SUMMARY.
(Erase heading not required.)

Army Form C. 2118.

VOLUME XXXVI OCTOBER 1918

Place	Date	Hour	Summary of Events and Information	Remarks and references to Appendices
FRANCE	1st		Bttn in line.	
			2/5 Ches Manchester Regt attacked BEAUREVOIR & TORCHAUX at Dawn supported by Bttn.	
			Chocans arm but Col R. NARING & 2 Lt EARLE near BEAUREVOIR CEMETERY	
			5 O.R. BEAUREVOIR CEMETERY was attacked by D Coy by dawn	
			BEAUREVOIR was taken by Battn & 7/5 Bn. at night	
			Heavy rain.	
MAP REF	4th		Bttn in line.	
MONTBREHAIN			Col HARING DC was wounded recovered at night. T was blind & 50MD injured & returned.	
			B. H. 1650 & B. & B.	
			Returned in line. Casualties to midnight 4. 20 O.R. 20 GENTZ&G.	
			Heavy enemy	
			Baltn took part in the advance with US Army at 5-10 am	
		3rd	PONCHAUX, BROCK FARM, FINAL OBJECT were taken. Wounded an by 1050	
		6th	Bn in line in reserve of SERAIN & PREMONT village at CATAUX WAY	
			Bttn was occupied with taking poll. Latter taken by enemy	
			LT CHARLESWORTH & 2LT WRIGHT wounded.	

SHEET 3

WAR DIARY
or
INTELLIGENCE SUMMARY.
(Erase heading not required.)

VOLUME XXXVI   OCTOBER 1918

Army Form C. 2118.

Place	Date	Hour	Summary of Events and Information	Remarks and references to Appendices
FRANCE	9th		Moved through out form forward to MARETZ WOOD when bivouacked	
			Day and by R.H. FLIER we went & eventually got on terms with	
			AMERICANS and our BDE. RIGHT when John was found	
			Country was being heavily shelled	
			Reaction slow	
			10th		Enemy had evacuated trenches on our front and NORTH of the RAIL	
			Bulk were in pursuing column, our party is left as American was retd.	
			well on RIGHT & a very slow force to be found on Left	
			ST GEORG & ST SOULLER extend	
			R.A.F. Volunteer kind	
			another 24 hrs. out good rest at night	
	15		Went to night in [illegible] when the [illegible] day and fresh	
			16:50 moved [illegible] [illegible] the men rolling on town all	
			went cheerful however	
			Battalion was billeted [illegible] into huts N ELINCOURT [illegible]	

Army Form C. 2118.

WAR DIARY
or
INTELLIGENCE SUMMARY

SHEET 4
VOLUME XXVI   OCTOBER 1918
(Erase heading not required.)

Place	Date	Hour	Summary of Events and Information	Remarks and references to Appendices
FRANCE	12		Day spent clearing up area of front line & front line.	
BUCQUOY			Total known casualties to Divisions 1st to 11th inclusive:-	
			OFFICERS KILLED 3 Other ranks 45	
			WOUNDED 6 " " 147	
			MISSING Nil " " 17	
			Total Prisoners taken during the operations. Officers 6. (Major 2nd Guards) Other Ranks 79. Field Guns 1. Trench Mortars 1.	A
			Lt Col Pilkington assumed command	
	13		Weather misty. Inspection of "B" & "C" & reliefs by M.O. etc officers	
			Battalion into billets in village	A
	14		Weather dull	
	15		Company training under O.C. Cos	A
			Weather dull	
	16		Company training & Lewis Gun training under O.C. Cos	A
			Lecture Lecture "Utility of Lewis Gun in the Battalion" by O.C. [?]	

WAR DIARY
or
INTELLIGENCE SUMMARY.
(Erase heading not required.)

Army Form C. 2118.

Place	Date	Hour	Summary of Events and Information	Remarks and references to Appendices
ELINCOURT	17th		The battalion under live honour notice to move. The day was spent in preparations for the move.	Sheet 57A NE 9/23 6/20
MAROIS	18th		The battalion moved by march route to MAROIS via MARETZ arriving in billets at about 1330 hours. The Brigade was in Divisional reserve. At 2300 hours orders were received to move at 0400 hours g.b.s. forward on the enemy who was believed to be contemplating a retirement.	g/23 Appendix II 9/23
S BENIN	19th		The battalion moved via HONNECHY – ESCAUFORT – to Q21A (Sheet 57 B). At 0700 hours the Order was received to move forward to Q22 6.2.0 via FASSIEU. At 1730 hours the battalion relieved the Scottish Horse S.D.K. Own in the front line in the LE CATEAU – BAZUEL Road. A+C Coy in front line; B Coy in Rear Reserve.	
In billets (Se/Benin)	20th		One platoon of C Company attacked at dawn the Gls of the River RICHEMONT from R 1 to L 31A in conjunction with the 2 Manchester and 9 Devons. The attack was not successful owing to the number of enemy machine guns entrenched by Artillery barrage.. 2/Lt J. LEA wounded. During the evening B Company moved up and to renew a portion of the front of C Company and of the 2 Devons killing machine men left	g/23

WAR DIARY or **INTELLIGENCE SUMMARY**

Army Form C. 2118.

Place	Date	Hour	Summary of Events and Information	Remarks and references to Appendices
POMMEREUIL	24th		Ref map POMMEREUIL FOREST 1/20.000 OISE CANAL 1/40.000 The Battalion was placed under an hours notice to move forward. In the evening the Battalion relieved the 1/7 Worcesters who in turn took over East of FONTAINE AU BOIS on the FONTAINE - ROBERSART Road. The Battalion being too Companies two Companies of 85 Bty. RFA, B.T.K. were in the front line. Patrols sent out. BN in touch with enemy. Large numbers of civilians in FONTAINE	(9K)
FONTAINE AU BOIS	25		Nodus Ben. HQ to central position in the village near the Church Fairly quiet day. Capt W. HORNSHER M.C. and 2/Lt L.J. POYNTER and ground reconned. Outside Bn HQ. Capt Rogers buried at POMMEREUIL. 2/L POYNTER Cross Road L II C. Patrols encountering with the enemy towards posts	
"	26"		Enemy artillery very active throughout day and night. Relieved in front line by 21st Manchester Rgt. No 2 Coy remained in support. B & D Coys back to R.H. No 1 Company withdrew to allow to FONTAINE. B & D withdrew to Cross road L II C. Quiet night	(9B)

Army Form C. 2118.

WAR DIARY
or
INTELLIGENCE SUMMARY.
(Erase heading not required.)

Instructions regarding War Diaries and Intelligence Summaries are contained in F.S. Regs., Part II. and the Staff Manual respectively. Title pages will be prepared in manuscript.

Place	Date	Hour	Summary of Events and Information	Remarks and references to Appendices
In Reserve	27.		Quiet day. Enemy aerial activity marked. Enemy attempted to raid area	Yes.
In Reserve	28"		Enemy aerial activity. Enemy artillery again active in back areas	Yes
"	29"		Fairly quiet day. Enemy artillery active.	
"	30		Relieved in reserve No 1 Coy by a Company of 7th Wiltshires No 2 Coy " " " 2nd Northumberland Fusiliers Bn HQ witheDRAWN	
	31		The Battalion marched to LE CATEAU and billeted in the MALTERIE near LE CATEAU Station arriving in billets at about 7 p.m. The day was spent in cleaning up, reorganising and absorbing drafts	Yes.

C.R. Pennington
Lieut Colonel
Cy 20th The Manchester Rgt
2nd/27th

APPENDIX I

20th Bn. THE MANCHESTER REGIMENT.

Narrative of the Fighting in which the Battalion was engaged from the 4th October to the 11th October, 1918.

Sheets MONTBREHAIN. 57B. S.W., 57B.SE. 1/20.000.

4th October. On the morning of the 4th October, the Battalion relieved a Battalion of the 5th Australian Brigade in the trench system opposite BEAUREVOIR and PONCHAUX. Battalion Headquarters was established in the sunken road at B.26.b.9.5. At 04.00, orders were received to attack and capture the villages of BEAUREVOIR and PONCHAUX together with the Trench system in B.11.c. The attack was timed to take place at 06.00, the 9th Devons on the left and the Australians on the right. The frontage allotted to the Battalion was from the road running N.E. through BEAUREVOIR(B.15.a, B.15.b, B.9.d, B.10.c,) inclusive to PONCHAUX inclusive. The objectives were the high ground N.E. of these villages.

'D'Company on the right were allotted the village of PONCHAUX; 'C'Company on the left, the portion of BEAUREVOIR allotted in the Battalion objective. 'A'Company was in reserve at Battalion H.Q.

[margin note: B Company in the centre the trench system in B 11 c and]

The Battalion attacked under the barrage at 0600 and succeeded in entering the villages of BEAUREVOIR and PONCHAUX, but owing to the heavy casualties received, the villages could not be held at 1310. An enemy counter-attack developed about noon and two platoons of 'A'Company were sent to reinforce the line. Meanwhile the counter-attack had been repulsed by Lewis Gun and Rifle fire. The Companies then established themselves on the general line - Windmill B.15.b.35.70 - B.16.b.3.3. - B.16.b.9.4 thence to a point west of GENEVE about B.17.d.3.8. where touch was obtained with the Australians. The low ground in B.16.b. was exposed to intense Machine Gun and Snipers fire from BEAUREVOIR and PONCHAUX and could not be occupied by troops. Considerable trouble was experienced from Snipers in B.17.b.8.6. and from the CEMETERY at B.16.b.9.6. The Commanding Officer (Lieut.Col.C.S.BURET,D.S.O.) went out to the line established to see the Companies at about noon and was hit in the leg by a Sniper. In the afternoon it was discovered that there was a considerable gap in the line from B.16.b.9.5 to the Windmill. It was impossible to establish troops along this length in daytime as they would be on a forward slope and exposed to heavy Machine Gun fire. Arrangements were made for this gap to be covered by a section of Machine Guns firing from B.20.d.7.5 until dark, when posts were established at B.155b.8.5 ; B.16.a.4.2., B.16.b.30.25. These posts, with the exception of the one at B.15.b.8.5. (which was moved nearer to the Mill) remained in position throughout the next day.

A post was also established at B.15.a.7.6 to watch the left and keep in touch with the troops on the left. The remaining platoon of 'A"Coy and 'A'Coy H.Q. was moved to the QUARRY at B.15.c.6.0 as Support to the left. During the day, the number of prisoners captured amounted to 2 Officers and 92 Other Ranks. Several Machine Guns and Automatic Rifles were captured and these were mounted in our line in preparation to meet a second enemy counter-attack, should it have occurred.

Our Casualties were :-

    Lieut.Col.C.S.BURT,D.S.O.)
    Capt.C.A.FORSYTH,M.M.   )
    Sec.Lieut.J.J.WILKINSON.   ) Wounded.
    Sec.Lieut.H.G.POULTON.   )
    Sec.Lieut.C.J.D.SEDDON.   )

Other Ranks   Killed - 24: Wounded - 85: Missing - 3.

The night of the 4/5th October was passed without incident. The enemy maintained a desultory fire on our lines. Our patrols went forward and located the enemy in BEAUREVOIR; the CEMETERY at B.16.b.9.8, the Station at B.16.b.2.8. and in PONCHAUX and GENEVE.

5th October. On the afternoon of the 5th, Capt.J.WARING,M.C. and Sec.Lieut.P.EARLE made a daylight Reconnaissance in the vicinity of the CEMETERY, bringing back to our lines five prisoners. Sec.Lieut.P.EARLE was wounded by a Sniper as he returned to our lines.
At 18.00 hours, orders were received to conform to the attack of the 75th Brigade on BEAUREVOIR and to secure the trenches in B.11.c. The barrage opened at 18.15, not allowing sufficient time to issue any orders to the Companies, consequently the opera-tion of this Battalion was delayed until some hours later.
On the night 5/6th, Patrols were sent out on the Battalion front, and the enemy was located in GENEVE and PONCHAUX. The Cemetery was occupied by us.
Casualties : Capt.J.WARING,M.C. - Wounded.
   Other Ranks. - Killed - 4. Wounded - 9.

6th October. At about 3.0 a.m. an attempt was made to capture the trench system in B.11.c. but the attempt was not successful. An enemy Machine Gun firing from about B.17.b.8.5. inflicting heavy casualties on the attacking party. *Fifteen enemy machine guns were later known to have been in B 11.c.*
At about 5.0 p.m. orders were received from the 7th Inf.Brigade to withdraw to the vicinity of B.20 on relief by the 9th Devons. The Battalion withdrew and established itself in the sunken road about B.20.b.0.4 where it remained during the night 6/7th.
Casualties:- Officers:- Capt.J.Waring, M.C. Killed.
   O.R.:- Killed - 10. Wounded - 11.
   Missing:- 5.

7th October. The Battalion was in the Sunken Road B.20.b.0.4 in reserve. The day was spent in cleaning Lewis Guns, S.A.A., Rifles etc., and in re-organising the Battalion into three Companies of effective strength.
'D'Company, which had suffered heavy casualties was split up between 'B' and 'C'Companies. On the night 7/8th October orders were received to detail 62 O.R. as carrying parties for the 100th M.G.C. This rendered the Companies weak in the attack on the next day.

8th October. The Battalion formed up on the ground in B.21.b: B.22.a: and B.23.a by 04.30 for the attack on PONCHAUX and the ground to the N.E. of the village. The frontage allotted to the Battalion was from the ESTREES - LE-CATEAU Road on the right to the line running through B.11.c.10.10 - C.1.a.5.0 on the left. The final objective was the line U.22 central to U.21.70.10. The Battalion front was allotted as follows :-
'A'Company to work along the southern sides of the main ESTREES - LE CATEAU Road to keep in touch with the 30th American Division on the right and to deal with

- 3 -

BRONX FARM, and SONIA, dropping a platoon at the first place and two platoons at SONIA.
'C' Company was detailed for the centre of the Battalion front and 'B' Company the left.
The role of the Battalion was to advance 800 yards in rear of the 21st Manchester Regiment and deal with any enemy. *and protect the right flank of the brigade.*
The attack commenced under the barrage at 0510.
In GENEVE a certain amount of mopping up was done by the Battalion ; about 30 prisoners being taken from a dugout, where the Railway crosses the main road at B.17.d.70.95. At BRONX FARM one German Officer and 35 O.R. were captured in the cellars under the farm. ✗ After passing this point the right of the Battalion came under heavy Machine Gun fire from FOAL COPSE and some scrub in C.8.a.4.7.
'A' Company attacked the COPSE and successfully dealt with the occupants, many being killed.. Some trench Mortars also in the Copse were captured. This creditable feat was performed in the face of very bitter enemy opposition. Meanwhile the fire from C.8.a.4.7 did not diminish so the services of a Tank were requisitioned and the spot was effectively cleared at about 11.30. Touch with the 30th American Division could not be obtained at this time. There were a few Americans around BRONX FARM but there was a large gap on our right extending East of FOAL COPSE. A protective flank was formed by 'A' Company and the whole Brigade attack halted on its first objective.
'B' Company on the left was still in rear of the 21st Manchester Regiment and 'C' Company in the centre was at SONIA.
On resumption of the attack to the second objective, 'B' Company followed the 21st Manchesters and assisted in forming a line on the final objective, meanwhile capturing an enemy Field Gun and a Howitzer, after passing through the 9th Devon. Regiment.
When the 21st Manchester Regt had gained its final objective the Battalion was established with two Companies in close support to the 21st Manchesters in U.27.a. 'A' Company and Battalion Headquarters being at U.26.d.10.10. the Americans having closed the gap on our right. Later 'A' Company was moved to a position in the Copse at U.27.b.2.4.6

    Casualties - Officers Wounded. Lieut.J.CHARLESWORTH.
                                        Sec.Lt.E.M.WRIGHT.
                                        Sec.Lt.L.H.SPENCER.
            Other Ranks. Killed - 4. Wounded 25.
                         Missing 6.

9th October.   Orders were received at about 01.00 to side step and relieve a Unit of the 30th American Division, taking over from the right boundary (a line U.29.a.37 - U.23.b.8.4. MAY COPSE) to the N.E. side of the building U.22.c.7.0 (inclusive) parallel to the LE CATEAU Road.
At 06.00 orders were received to concentrate in U.22.d. and at about 08.00 the Battalion moved in accordance with instructions to U.18.d.8.8. on the western edge of MARETZ WOOD. Here a halt was made until the morning of the 10th October.
    Casualties - Other Ranks - Wounded 7.

10th October.   On the morning of the 10th October the Battalion, moved forward at 05.30 on the right of the 7th Brigade which was in Divisional Reserve. The 74th and 75th Brigades were detailed to carry out the attack and capture the high ground to the East of LE CATEAU. The line of advance was parallel to the LE CATEAU Road from V.5.a.0.0 on the South side of the Railway. The role of the Battalion was to keep touch with the Americans on the right and watch that flank. The attack progressed favourably until the valley running through Q.25 central was reached.
Here the Battalion halted to conform to the general attack and observe the correct distance in rear of the 11th

Sherwood Forresters (74th Bde.) Word was received about 08.30 that the Americans who were outside the village of ST.SOUPLET were expecting a counter-attack from that direction. Accordingly, a defensive flank was formed with two Companies on the high ground Q.31.b. Q.26.d. The third Company was in the sunken road at Q.26.a. and c. Considerable enemy shelling was experienced by the Companies and Battalion Headquarters but no enemy attack materialised, and later the two Companies were withdrawn to the valley at Q.25 central. At 14.30 the attack of the 74th Brigade was resumed under a barrage and the enemy opposition encountered by them at ST.BENIN was overcome. In accordance with orders, the Battalion was disposed in the valley Q.25.central with look out posts on the high ground in Q.25.b., Q.26.a.and c. Battalion H.Q. was on the North side of the railway embankment at Q.19.c.7.0. The role of the Battalion was to watch the right flank of the 74th and 75th Brigades in co-operation with the 9th Devons. The night 10/11th October passed without incident.

    Casualties - Officers. Lieut.K.R.WOLLASTON. Killed.
              Other Ranks. Wounded - 7.

11th October. The morning of the 11th October found the Battalion in the same position. The attitude of the enemy was quiet on the whole.
During the morning orders for relief by the 50th Division were received and the Battalion was withdrawn from its position at 19.30 on receipt of instructions, and moved to Billets in ELINCOURT via HONNECHY and MARETZ.
The Battalion was established in Billets at 23.00 hours.
    Casualties - Other Ranks - Wounded. 3.

During these operations after Lt Col C S Burt was wounded at noon on the 2nd Oct, the battalion was commanded by Major J S Gemmel M.C.

14.10.18.

                        C R Pillington Lieut.Colonel,
                        Cdg.20th Bn.THE MANCHESTER REGIMENT.

SECRET.

APPENDIX II

20th BATTALION THE MANCHESTER REGIMENT.

NARRATIVE OF EVENTS FROM 18th OCTOBER to 30th OCTOBER, 1918.

18th Oct. The Battalion left Elincourt and moved via Maretz to Marois, arriving in billets about 1300 hours.

19th Oct. The Battalion moved at 0400 hours through Honnechy -Escaufort to the ground Q.21,d, West of St. Benin. (Maps 57B SE & NE). At 0700 hours an order was received to proceed to the ground Q.22.b.2.0. via Fassieu. At this place a halt was made for dinners and teas. The Commanding Officer and Adjutant went forward to the H.Q. Scottish Horse, (50th Divn) in the Railway Station Le Cateau to arrange details of relief. The Battalion moved off at 1610 hours via Le Quennelet Grange and relieved the Scottish Horse, A and C Companies in the front line from R.1.d.8.3. to Q.6.b.6.0. B Company and Bn. H.Q. dug into the bank on the road Q.11.d.5.0.

20th Oct, In conjunction with the 21st Manchesters, an attack by one platoon was made from the line of the road R.1.d.0.3. to Q.6.b,6.0. under a creeping barrage. The objective was the line of the Richemont Stream from the Mill R.2.a.1.5. inclusive to Jacques

Ref Map Mill exclusive, as Battalion frontage. The form of the attack
Forest   was three patrols, each consisting of 8 all ranks in each patrol.
1/20000 The 66th Divn. were to co-operate on the left, and the 75 Bde. on the right of the 21st Manchesters. As soon as the patrols moved forward they came under very heavy fire from machine guns from the left and front, and could make no progress after about 150 yds. The Officer in charge of the patrols was wounded at the outset and many casualties occurred in the patrols. The enemy also fired on our wounded, and is known to have killed four in this way. The remnants of the patrols were able to get back at dusk, and those of our wounded still out in front, were brought in. On the night of the 20th October, the battle front was extended to the left by bringing in B company to the front line and taking over from the 5th Inniskilling Fusiliers (66th Divn), the portion of the line Q.6.b.6.0. to Q.6.a8.3. One Company of the 9th Devon Regt. was placed under the orders of O.C. 20th Manchesters to be used in case of counter attack, and was located at Q.11.b.4.2. One section of the M.G.C. was also allotted for defensive purposes and placed on the Northern bank of the Railway cutting.

21 Oct. A fairly quiet day. There was a certain amount of shelling around the Railway cutting and Battalion Headquarters. B Company were withdrawn to the Railway cutting. The post at Q.6.b.7.7. remained in position.

22 Oct. During the night 22/23 Oct. the post of B Company at Q.6.b.7.7. was withdrawn to the cutting.

23rd Oct. At 0120 hours the Battalion, in conjunction with the remainder of the 7th Brigade and with the 18th Divn. on the left attacked under a barrage. The Battalion right boundary was a straight line from a point on the road 200 yds. N.W. of the road junction R.1.c. 55.50 to the junction of the track and river L.31.d.2.0. thence a straight line to the road junction L.26.b,7.0. The Battalion left boundary was K.36,d.6.0. - Moulin du Garde (inclusive) - Copse L.25.b, - L.26.a. (incl) - L.20.d.4.5. - thence 300 yds. N.W. of edge of Bois L'Eveque. The objective was the portion of the following line lying between the above mentioned boundaries:- L.33.d.31. - Foresters House (L.27.d.29) N.E. edge of Pommereuil - extreme west corner of wood L.20.d.45,

NARRATIVE OF EVENTS 18th Oct. to 30th Oct. Contd.

where touch was to be made with 18th Divn. Compass bearings had been taken to assist in the maintenance of direction. The attack was carried out on a two Company frontage with one Company in reserve. Thirty other ranks were detailed to assist the R.E. in bridging the Richemont Stream on the portion to be crossed by the Battalion. Owing to the darkness, mist and smoke fumes from the shells, it was impossible to see the progress of the attack. The Officer i/c the bridging party reported on his return after completing the bridging, that our men were well over the stream, and had not waited for the bridges, but had pushed on, wading through the stream. For some considerable time after zero hour no authentic news could be obtained concerning the attack. Runners coming back had been knocked out and signal communication, even by lamp, was an impossibility owing to the smoke. Wounded coming back reported our men well ahead, (one wounded signaller at 0300 reported that his Company were entering the village of Pommereuil when he was hit. This was confirmed later by the O.C. left Company returning wounded. He had been hit when with his Company at L.26.b.0.1. There was still a considerable amount of rifle and M.G. fire from L.31.a & c and Garde Mill was in the hands of the enemy at 0530 hours. Therefore the reserve Company was disposed along the original front on the Le Cateau - Bazuel Road ready to move forward and deal with pockets of the enemy who evidently remained. When day broke the reserve Company was ordered to work round in small parties through R.1.a., L.31.c and b to clear up pockets of the enemy, who surrendered at once on finding themselves surrounded. Battalion H.Q. moved up through Becqueriaux and L.32.c to Pommereuil where the two Companies had consolidated and dug in on their objective, having had severe casualties. The bulk of the casualties had occurred in the orchards about L.32.a central, the enemy being very strong in the hedges facing west.

Meanwhile the 75th and 74th Infy. Bdes. had passed through and continued the attack on the 2nd and 3rd objectives.

At 1000 hours the Battalion was withdrawn into Billets in Pommereuil.

24 Oct.

Ref Map Forest 1/20000

On the 24th Oct. the Battalion was placed under an hour's notice to move forward in necessary. At 0600 hours the Commanding Officer and Adjutant went forward to Fontaine au Bois to take over a portion of the front line from the 1/7 Worcestershire Regt. 75th Bde. The Battalion followed by route, Tilleuls Fm. - Garage Corner. On relief, the Battalion (consisting now of two Compabies only) held a frontage by a line of posts through G.8.b.20, - G.2.d.2.8. - North side of road running through G.2.a to farm G.2.a 2.5. where touch was gained with the 7th Queens, 18th Divn. The 9th Devons were on our right. One Company of the 21st Manchesters was placed at the disposal of O.C. 20th Manchesters as reserve and dug in at G.1.d.7.7. Bn. H.Q. was in house at Bout du Monde L.6.c.0.9. Patrols were sent out and located the enemy in the hedges at G.2.b.2.2. to G.2.a.8.3.

25 Oct

Battalion H.Q. moved to a more central position in the house G.7.b.4.9. near Church of Fontaine. Again in the evening patrols worked along from Les Grands Chenes forward to the main Landrecies road at G.2.b.3.2. where they came under heavy fire from M.Gs at G.2.b.1.4. Patrols also drew fire from hedges at G.2.a.8.3, and also from cross roads A.26.c,9.1.

26 Oct.

The battalion was relieved in the line by the 21st Manchesters and passed in Brigade Reserve. Battalion H.Q. moved back to Cross Roads L.11.c.5.2. No 1 Company moved to cellars about L.21.c.9.7. No 2 Company withdrew on relief to dug-positions at G.1.d.7.7. and acted as reserve to O.C. 21 Manchester Regt,

27 Oct. Fairly quiet day: Considerable enemy aerial and artillery activity.

28 Oct. No 1 Company came under the orders of O.C. 9th Devons as reserve, No. 2 Company coming back under orders of O.C. 20th Manchesters.

29 Oct. Quiet day. Enemy aerial activity marked.

30 Oct. The Battalion was relieved in Brigade reserve. No. 1 Company was relieved By A Company of the 7th Wiltshire Regt. (50th Divn) and No. 2 Company by a Company of the 2nd Northumberland Fusiliers (50th Division,

1.11.18

C R Pennington Lieut-Colonel,
Cdg. 20th Bn. The Manchester Regiment.

20th Battalion The Manchester Regiment.

NOMINAL ROLL OF OFFICERS as on 31-10-18.

Colonel.
   Lieut.Colonel C.R.Pilkington, C.M.G, ... With Battalion.

MAJORS.
   J.S.Gemmell, M.C. .... With Battalion.

CAPTAINS.
   F.Nicholls. .... With Battalion.
   A.G.N.Dixey M.C, ... In hospital.

LIEUTENANTS.
   G.F.S.Brownlow, (A/Capt)..............................On course.
   H.S.Painter M.C. ....On leave U.K.
   E.W.Shaw ....Area Commdt. Serain.
   T.M.Lees ....In hospital.
   E.H.Shackle M.C. ....On course.
   H.P.Vellmer ....With Battalion.

SECOND LIEUTENANTS.
   D.Kitchen ....With Battalion.
   H.S.Latham ....With Battalion.
   J.Kilroe ....In Hospital - Italy.
   L.H.Spencer ....With Battalion.
   G.D.Ramsay ....In Hospital,
   J.T.Walley ....With Battalion,
   E.Crossley M.C. ....With Battalion.
   J.Isherwood ....With Battalion.
   J.Elder. ....With Battalion.
   H.Branham ....With Battalion.

MEDICAL OFFICER.
   Capt. P.E.Carroll. (R.A.M.C.) ....With Battalion.

ADJUTANT.
   Captain G.B.Dempsey. M.C. ....With Battalion.

QUARTERMASTER.
   Capt. & Q.M. T.J.McKenna ....With Battalion.

31-10-18.
                                                                 C.R.Pilkington Lieut-Colonel,
                                            Cdg. 20th Bn. The Manchester Regiment.

20th Bn. THE MANCHESTER REGIMENT.

CASUALTIES DURING THE MONTH OF OCTOBER, 1918.

OFFICERS.

T/Lieut.COL. C.S.Burt, D.S.O. (1st S.Staffs. Regt). Attd. 20 M.R.	Wounded	4.10.18.
Capt. C.A.Forsyth, M.M.	Wounded	4.10.18.
2/Lieut. H.G.Poulton	Wounded	4.10.18.
2/Lieut. J.J.Wilkinson	Wounded	4.10.18.
2/Lieut. C.J.D.Sedden.	Wounded	4.10.18.
2/Lieut. P. Earle.	Wounded	5.10.18.
Capt. J. Waring M.C.	Killed in Action	6.10.18.
Lieut. J.Charlesworth	Wounded	8.10.18.
2/Lieut. E.M.Wright.	Wounded	8.10.18.
Lieut. K.R.Wollaston.	Killed in Action	10.10.18.
Capt. G.W.L.Pritchard.	Killed in Action	23.10.18.
2/Lieut. G.S.Walker.	Killed in Action	23.10.18.
2/Lieut. A. Hülme.	Killed in Action	23.10.18.
Capt. H.S.Bagshaw M.C.	Wounded	23.10.18.
2/Lieut J. Lea.	Wounded	20.10.18.
2/Lieut. R. O. Garside	Wounded	23.10.18.
Capt. W.H.Bowsher M.C.	Died of Wounds.	25.10.18.
2/Lieut L.J.Poynter	Died of Wounds.	25.10.18.

OTHER RANKS.

Killed in action .... 78.

Wounded .... 223.

Missing .... 27.

Sick .... 60.
(Evacuations)

1.11.18.

CR Pickington Lieut-Colonel,
Cdg. 20th Bn. The Manchester Regiment.

20th BATTALION THE MANCHESTER REGIMENT

REINFORCEMENTS RECEIVED DURING THE MONTH OF OCTOBER, 1918.

OFFICERS.

	Date of Arrival.
Lieut.Colonel C.R.Pilkington C.M.G.	11.10.18.
Lieut. H.P.Vollmer.	27.10.18.
T/Sec.Lieut. G.S.Walker.	13.10.18.
T/Sec.Lieut. A. Hulme.	13.10.18.
T/Sec,Lieut. J. Lea.	13.10.18.
2/Lieut. Branham H.	13.10.18.
T/Capt. H.S.Bagshaw M.C.	13.10.18.

OTHER RANKS.

105	O.R. joined Battalion	10.10.18.
21	" " "	17.10.18.
2	" " "	21.10.18.
11	" " "	24.10.18.
123	" " "	24.10.18.
97	" " "	25.10.18.
9	" " "	30.10.18.

1.11.18.

Lieut.Colonel,
Cdg, 20th Bn. The Manchester Regiment,

Secret.

96/37

War Diary

of

20th Battn The Manchester Regiment

From 1st November, 1918 To 30th November, 1918.

Volume 37.

J Hmmett Major.
Cdg 20th Battn The Manchester Regt.

Sheet I.

Army Form C. 2118.

WAR DIARY
or
INTELLIGENCE SUMMARY.
(Erase heading not required.)

Volume XXXVII. November 1918.

Place	Date	Hour	Summary of Events and Information	Remarks and references to Appendices
FRANCE	1st		Battalion billeted in the MALTERIE, LE CATEAU. Day spent in absorption of reinforcements and reorganisation of Companies.	A.D.
	2nd		LE CATEAU. Day spent in training Lewis Gunners, and Companies in attack formation.	App. I
	3rd		The Battalion moved from LE CATEAU at 1618 hours and marched to POMMEREUIL and bivouacked for the night in an area in L.27 near that village. Battalion H.Q. was established in the FORESTERS' HOUSE L.27.d.3.9. "B" Echelon and Transport Lines remained at LE CATEAU.	App.
Map. FOREST 1/10,000	4th		The Battalion, as part of 7th Brigade was in Divisional Reserve during an attack carried out by the 74th and 75th Brigades, in conjunction with troops on Left and Right, with a view to breaking through the enemy defences on the SAMBRE- OISE CANAL, and PETITE HELPE River. Zero hour was 0615 hours. The attack progressed favourably in spite of opposition on the Canal, and many prisoners of the JAGER Regts were captured. At 1350 hours orders received to move to MALGARNI via Road Junction L.27.d.1.9. The Battalion moved at	App.
Map. Sh. 57A 1/40,000				

Sheet 2.

WAR DIARY
or
INTELLIGENCE SUMMARY.
(Erase heading not required.)

Army Form C. 2118.

November 1918

Place	Date	Hour	Summary of Events and Information	Remarks and references to Appendices
FRANCE	4th	1450 hours	and proceeded to L.24 a. 0.9 where orders were received to march via HAPPEGARBES to LANDRECIES where a defensive line was to be taken up along the Railway in conjunction with the 21st Manchester Regt. The line taken up by the Battalion was from	
Map Sheet 57A	1/40,000.		the Road (exclusive) G.16.d.5.3 to G.17 Central. "A" and "C" Coys in the front line with B and D Coys in support. Battn. H.Q was established in the house at G.16.d.6.3. Later moving to the Chateau G.17.c.3.1. There were many large buildings on fire in the area occupied by the Battn	300
		5 AM	The advance was continued via LANDRECIES - LE PRESEAU (H14a) - OLD MILL des PRES (H & L.9.6) to RUE du LIEUTENANT, where the Battalion dug in on the North and South sides of the MARBAIX - LES MARBAIXES Road, in support to the 13th Durham Light Infantry (74th Brigade). Weather very wet.	300
	6th		The Advance was continued. The Battalion was ordered to form the Advanced guard to the 7th Inf. Brigade, and was allotted One Troop 12th Lancers (less 1 Section), One Company R.E. (less one Section) and two Armoured Cars. The objective was a line through the	Appendix III

Army Form C. 2118.

WAR DIARY Sheet 3
or
INTELLIGENCE SUMMARY.
(Erase heading not required.)

November 1918.

Place	Date	Hour	Summary of Events and Information	Remarks and references to Appendices
FRANCE	6th		Crossroads in I2a to Crossroads in J7 central. The Vanguard was found by B.Coy with "C" Coy in close support, and D and A Companies provided the Main Guard. The line of Advance was Road fork H11c – RUE des HAIES – BASSE NOYELLES – TAISNIERES –	
Map Sheet 57A 1/40,000			LE CATTIAUX – DOMPIERRE. The Battalion passed through the Outpost Line, held by 21st Manchesters at 0630 hours. At 0810 hours the Advanced Guard was held up by Machinegun and Rifle fire at BASSE NOYELLES (about I1 a 8.8). This opposition was soon overcome and the advance resumed at 0850 hours. At 0930 opposition was met with at the Crossroads TAISNIERES from M/c Guns and trench mortars and enfilade fire was experienced from an Orchard about I&L. A stiff fight about this place resulted in about 15 of the enemy being killed and 13 captured, with only slight casualties ourselves. On reaching the bridge over the river at I3a, the "Point" was just too late to save it from being blown up, but the man who fired the charge was shot	Appendix III Appendix

Army Form C. 2118.

WAR DIARY
or
INTELLIGENCE SUMMARY.
(Erase heading not required.)

Sheet 4

November 1918.

Place	Date	Hour	Summary of Events and Information	Remarks and references to Appendices
FRANCE	6th		The whole Battalion was across the river at 1150 hours and the advance continued. In LE CATTIAUX enemy riflemen who had been harassing us were killed or captured, and at the farm at I.5.c.3.5 a Trench Mortar Battery and two anti-tank limbers were captured.	
Map Sheet 57A 1/40,000.		at about 1320 hours.	By 1350 hours the ridge I.5.a – I.6.a had been taken but enemy was seen digging in on Ridge at I.6.d in strength. A Reserve Platoon was ordered to try and outflank the enemy who also and some of his troops to attack over left flank. Our troops however, were too firmly established and the enemy hastily withdrew, under heavy fire. Enemy shelling was heavy round knoll at I.5.c.3.5 and in valley at I.5.a. The ridge at I.6.d. still gave trouble, but as the South of the village was clear, a flanking movement was made, which was entirely successful. Many by the enemy were found in the streets of DOMPIERRE and captured; and the machine gunners on the ridge at I.6.d were dealt with. Some of them found wearing Red Cross brassards were finally shot.	VII Appendices

WAR DIARY

Sheet 5

INTELLIGENCE SUMMARY.

(Erase heading not required.)

November 1918

Place	Date	Hour	Summary of Events and Information	Remarks and references to Appendices
FRANCE.	6th		The capture of the village was completed by 19.30 hours and the vanguard took up a line of posts along the road East of DOMPIERRE. Later in the evening pushing over the railway line ahead of about 50 prisoners was taken in the village together with many machine guns. Early in the afternoon, enemy had blown up Railway bridge J.a.1.4 and River bridge J.a.5.5. Bridge at J.a.4 reported by Civilians to be mined. Battalion HQ was established in a house on south side of Mulhurch. Total prisoners taken during the day was about 30. Our casualties: Killed 4 OR. Wounded: 2nd Lt J ELDER and 17 OR. Weather throughout the day being wet.	
MAP Sheet 57A				
1/40000.				
	7th		Patrols pushed out from outpost line in the early morning failed to locate the enemy. The advance was continued, the 2nd Manchesters kept being ordered to find the advanced guard. 10pm passing through Outpost line at 08.00 hours. At about 10.00 hours, the Battalion, As part of the main body marched along the road 2 kilos NE of DOMPIERRE but the Column was checked at a point 2 kilos NE of DOMPIERRE	Appendix III

Army Form C. 2118.

WAR DIARY
Sheet 6
or
INTELLIGENCE SUMMARY.
(Erase heading not required.)

November 1918

Place	Date	Hour	Summary of Events and Information	Remarks and references to Appendices
FRANCE	7th		and no further progress was made up to 1615 hours when the Battalion was ordered to withdraw and return to Billets in DOMPIERRE. Billets reached at 1900 hours. HQ in M. Mongers house adjoining Church.	
Sht 61 A 1/40000	8th		Battalion moved at 1000 hours by route march via HUGEMONT - MARBAIX - MAROILLES - to LANDRECIES, arriving about 1500 hours. The old French BIRON Barracks, much damaged by shellfire, was allotted to the Battalion as a billet.	Appendices III
	9th		Day spent in cleaning up Billet, Equipment &c and checking deficiencies.	
	10th		Party of 10 Officers and 100 O.R. detailed for work in cleaning up streets in the town. 1100 hours Parade Service in Theatre. During the afternoon the President of the French Republic visited the town.	
	11th		Two Companies detailed to work cleaning up and repairing HAPPEGARBES - LANDRECIES road. Remainder Bathing & training.	

WAR DIARY
INTELLIGENCE SUMMARY

Army Form C. 2118.

Sheet ?
November 1918

Place	Date	Hour	Summary of Events and Information	Remarks and references to Appendices
FRANCE. Sheet 67A HUCCOO.	11th		Official notification of the cessation of hostilities at 1100 hours received. Weather fine.	App
	12th		Battalion on working parties. Bathing and training. At 1100 hours the Divisional Commander inspected billets and the men at work. Weather fine.	App
	12th		Battalion moved from LANDRECIES at 1030 hours via HAPPEGARBES to billets in POMMEREUIL, arriving about 1230 hours. Batt'n HQ established in house about L26d.9.1. Weather fine.	App IX
	14th		POMMEREUIL. Day spent in Company training, cleaning up billets, and clearing up and repairing roads in vicinity.	App
	15th		POMMEREUIL. Company training and clearing up billets and Roads. At 1600 hours the Divisional Commander entertained the officers of the Division who took part in the recent operations to tea, in the Theatre. Weather fine.	App
	16th		LE CATEAU. Weather fine	App
	16th		POMMEREUIL. Training and fatigues as far 15th.	App
	17th		Voluntary services in concert room. Weather fine.	App

Army Form C. 2118.

Sheet 8

WAR DIARY
or
INTELLIGENCE SUMMARY.
(Erase heading not required.)

November 1918.

Instructions regarding War Diaries and Intelligence Summaries are contained in F. S. Regs., Part II. and the Staff Manual respectively. Title pages will be prepared in manuscript.

Place	Date	Hour	Summary of Events and Information	Remarks and references to Appendices
POMMEREUIL	18th 19th		Companies training 0900 to 1200 hours	Reo
	20th		A & B Companies commenced salvage operations in Headquarters L27 & L28 working from 0900 hours to 1600 hours. C & D Coys training as usual. Divnl Commander saw the Battalion at work. Weather fine & bright.	Reo
Sheet 57A 1/40000		21st	A B & C Coys continued salvage operations in same area. D Coy training. Bathing to Divisional Baths. Weather fine.	Reo
		22nd	C & D Coys continued salvage operations. Divnl Baths allotted to A & B Coys. Weather fine.	Reo
		23rd	Salvage operations continued by A & B Coys. Voluntary Services in Concert Room POMMEREUIL 1015 hours. Weather fine.	Reo
		24th		Reo
		25th	A & B Coys continued salvage operations. C & D Coys usual training. Divisional Baths for details. 1 O.R. slightly injured while detonating a German Grenade.	Reo
		26th	C & D Coys - salvage operations. A & B Coys training	Reo

WAR DIARY
or
INTELLIGENCE SUMMARY.
(Erase heading not required.)

Sheet 9
November 1918
Army Form C. 2118.

Place	Date	Hour	Summary of Events and Information	Remarks and references to Appendices
POMMEREUIL Sheet 57A 1/40,0-00	27th		The Whole Battalion continued Salvage operations up to 1300 hours. A & B Coys allotted Divnl Baths in Afternoon.	fine
	28th		Salvage operations continued by all Companies. Work in the area ceased at 1200 hours. Weather very wet.	fine
Map VALENCIENNES 1/100,000	29th		Battalion moved from POMMEREUIL at 0914 hours and marched via MONTAY - NEUVILLY STATION - BRIASTRE to Billets in QUIÉVY, arriving about 1300 hours. Weather Dull with occasional rain.	fine
	30th		Day spent in cleaning up Billets and Billeting Area. Weather fine.	fine

J. Mann M
Major
for Lt. Col. 20th Bn. The Manchester Regt.

War Diary APPENDIX. I

SECRET.   Copy No. 12
                 20th Bn. THE MANCHESTER REGIMENT.
                          ORDER No. 153.
Ref.Maps : FOREST 1/20.000
           Sheets 57a N.W. 57b. N.E.

1.   The Battalion will move to Bivouac area in the vicinity of POMMEREUIL tomorrow 3rd November.   'B'Echelon Details will remain in the present area.   Numbers will be notified later.

2.   Parade ready to move off at 1555 hours.
Order of March : H.Q., 'A', 'B', 'C', 'D'Coys.   The head of the column will be opposite the Northern end of the MALTERIE. Coys will be in column of route on the right of the road facing North. On the march 100 yards between Companies will be maintained. Lewis Gun Limbers will follow their respective Companies.   The 'A'Echelon vehicles and Mess Cart will march in rear of the Battalion maintaining the usual intervals.   A Lewis Gunner will be in rear of each L.G.Limber with guns ready for action.   Cookers will proceed in rear of 'A' Echelon.

3.   Dress - Full marching order with Steel Helmets. Blankets will be dumped at the Q.M.Stores by 1200 hours.

4.   Advance Party consisting of C.Q.M.Sergts and Corpl.STOTT will report to the Staff Captain at the Military Cemetery, POMMEREUIL at 1300 hours.   Parade at Orderly Room 1130 hours to receive tents and area allotment.   Tents and Bivouacs will not be erected until dusk.   Tools etc. will be issued in the new area.

5.   Officer's Kits, Mess Boxes, and Dixies, will be dumped at the Q.M.Stores by 1430 hours.   Mess Boxes will be carried forward by the Mess Cart.

6.   Transport Lines will remain in present position until further orders.

7.   The Billets will be left thoroughly clean.

8.   Cookers and Mess Cart will be returned to 'B'Echelon later. The Q.M. will arrange to send up rations for the 4th November.

Issued at 11.18 p.m.   Captain & Adjutant.
2nd November, 1918.

               Copy No.1. C.O.   No.7. Q.M.
                    2. H.Q.Mess.   8. Transport Sergt.
                    3. O.C. 'A'Coy.   9. H.Q.Sergts.
                    4.   "   'B' ..   10. File.
                    5.   "   'C' ..   11 & 12. War Diary.
                    6.   "   'D' ..

APPENDIX. II

SECRET.
20th BATTALION 6
THE MANCHESTER

20th Bn. THE MANCHESTER REGIMENT.

Ref.Maps - 1/20.000 57A.N.E. and 57B.N.W.

No. 674
Date

1. The 25th Division with the 32nd Division on its right and the 30th Division on its left will take part in an operation on a large scale with a view to breaking through the enemy defences on a date and at an hour to be notified later.

2. The barrage opens at ZERO on the line G.20.b.4.0 - G.9.c.1.9

3. The 75th Infantry Brigade will capture the first objective (RED Line) and the Outpost Line beyond (Dotted RED). The 1/5th.Gloster Regt on the right and the 1/8th Warwick Regt. on the left are attacking as far as the Canal, the 1/8th Worcester Regt is following up the attack, forcing the passage of the Canal and establishing, firstly the RED Line, and then the Outpost Line beyond (Dotted RED) If practicable, troops of the two leading Battalions will cross the Canal first and form a covering party for the 1/8th Worcester Regt, whilst effecting the crossing.

The 74th Infy.Brigade is pushing through the 75th Infy.Bde at about ZERO plus 7 hours (Forcing the passage of the Canal if the 75th Bde has been unable to carry this out) and pushing on to the attack on the GREEN Line. The 11th Sherwood Foresters are carrying out this attack supported by the 9th Yorks Regt.
The 13th Durham L.I. will be in Brigade Reserve.

4. The 7th Infy.Brigade (less two Companies 21st Manchesters) is in Divisional Reserve. The two Companies 21st Manchester Regt. under a Senior Officer will, under orders of G.O.C., 75th Infy.Bde. be detailed to mop up the area between grid line through G.20 Central - G.21 Central and the right flank of the 75th Brigade, during its advance (G.20.b.45 - G.22.a.0.0.) Liaison Posts will be established with 32nd Division at G.21.b.40 (on road) G.22.a.0.0 (on Railway).

5. Arrangements for crossing Canal and LA PETITE HELPE River are being made by C.R.E.

6. Light Signals will be used as follows :-
    5 White Lights - Leading Battalion has crossed Canal.
    5 Red Lights - Red Line reached.

7. Tanks will assist in advance.
Smoke Screens will be provided by Artillery, Aeroplanes, and Special Company R.E. Armoured Cars will also co-operate.

8. Line of advance of the Division will be :-
POMMEREUIL - CHAPEL Cross Roads (L.29.a.5.2) - MALGARNI - Road junction L.18.a.7.9 - Road junction G.19.b.7.9 - G.14.c.8.4. - G.20.b.0.6. - G.15.d.6.4.
C.R.E. will make a track from L.24.c.4.9 - G.20.b.0.5 fit for Limbers so that MALGARNI may be avoided. Line of Communication will be the same as the line of Advance.

9. Contact planes will call for flares at ZERO plus 5 hours, ZERO plus 6 hours and at 1400, and 1600 hours. Counter attack planes will patrol the front from DAWN to dusk. In the event of a counter attack developing this plane will drop white parachute lights over the centre of the hostile troops.

Issued at 950 a.m.
3rd November, 1918.
                                        Captain & Adjutant.

        Copy No.1. O.C. 'A'Coy.
             2. "   'B' "
             3. "   'C' "
             4. "   'D' "
             5. Q.M.
             6 & 7. War Diary.

APPENDIX III

SECRET.   20th Bn. THE MANCHESTER REGIMENT.

Narrative of Operations from 3rd November to 8th November, 1918.

Ref. Maps. Forest 1/10000
57a 1/40000.

3rd Nov. The Battalion moved from LE CATEAU at 1618 hours on the
3rd Nov. and marched via POMMEREUIL to an area allotted in
L.27.a near that village.

Map
FOREST   The Battalion, as part of the 7th Brigade, was in Divisional
1/10000.   Reserve during an attack carried out by the 74th and 75th Infy.
Bdes., in conjunction with troops on the left and right, with a
view to breaking through the enemy defences on the SAMBRE –
OISE CANAL, and PETIT HELPE River on the 4th Nov.
Battalion H.Q. was established in the FORRESTER'S HOUSE L.27d.3.9.
"B" Echelon and Transport Lines remained at LE CATEAU.

4th Nov. Zero hour on the 4th November was 0615 hours for the 25th Divn.
The attack apparently went well, though much opposition was encountered on the CANAL. Many prisoners of the JAGER Regiment
MAP   were captured. At 1350 hours orders were received to move to
57a 1/40000 ALGARBI via road Junction L.27d.1.9. The Battalion moved at
1450 hours and proceeded to L.34a.9.9. where orders were
received to march via HAPPEGARBES to LANDRECIES, where a
defensive line was to be taken up along the railway in conjunction
with the 21st Manchester Regiment. The 9th Devons were sent
forward to G.24 to assist in the defensive positions.
The line taken by the Battalion was from the road (exclusive) in
G.16.d.5.5. to G.17 central.
Battalion H.Q. was in the house G.17.d.6.3. and later moved
to the Chateau G.17c.30.10.

5th Nov. The advance was continued the following day via LANDRECIES –
LE PRESEAU (H 19a) – LA BLANCHISSERIE – (H 13d) – CATILLON FARM
(H 14a) – OLD MILL des PRES (H.8.b.7.6.) to RUE de LIEUTENANT,
where the Battalion dug in in support to the 13th D.L.Y. (74th
Brigade) on the North and South sides of the MARCILLES road.
H.Q. was with the H.Q. 9th Devons in a house about H.10.c.4.4.

6th Nov. The advance was continued on the morning of 6th Nov. The
× Advance   Battalion,× together one troop 12th Lancers (less one section),
guard to the one Company R.E. (less one section), one armoured car passed
7 Brigade   through the outpost line held by the 21st Manchester Regt. at
0630 hours.
The objective was a line through the cross roads in J.2a. – to
cross roads in J.7 central. The 50th Divn. on the left and
the 74th Bde. on the right advanced at the same hour. The
vanguard consisted of "B" Company under Capt. F.Nicholls,
"C" Company, under 2/Lt. D.Kitchen were in close support. "D"
and "A" Companies provided the mainguard under 2/Lt. Isherwood
and 2/Lt. Walley respectively. The line of advance was road
fork H.11c – RUE des HAIES – BASSE NOYELLES – TAISNIERES –
LE GATTIAUX – DOMPIERRE.
At 0810 hours the advance guard was held up at BASSE NOYELLES
about I.1.a.8.8. by M.G. fire and by rifle fire. This
opposition was soon overcome by use of flanking fire from
Lewis Guns and the attack pressed on at 0850 hours. At 0930
hours much opposition was met at the cross roads TAISNIERES from
M.Gs and Trench Mortars and enfilade fire was experienced from
an orchard about I.8.b. A stiff fight took place about this
latter point which resulted in some casualties to us, but about
15 enemy were killed and thirteen captured. On reaching the
bridge over the river at I.3a the point of the advance guard
was just too late to save it from being blown up. However,
the man who blew it up was shot. The whole Battalion was
across the river at 1150 hours. The bridge was not sufficiently
destroyed to prevent Infantry and pack mules crossing over, and
so the attack was pushed on. Enemy riflemen who harassed us
in LE GATTIAUX were killed or captured, and at the farm at
I.5.c.3.5. the trench mortar battery was captured together with
two anti-tank limbers at about 1230 hours.
At 1350 hours the ridge at I.5d – I.6a had been taken, but

Narrative of Operations 3rd Nov. to 8th Nov. 1918, (contd).

the enemy were seen digging in on ridge at I.6d, in strength. Enemy shelling was heavy around farm I.5c.3.5. and in valley I.5d. A reserve platoon was sent to try and outflank the enemy. The enemy also sent some of his troops to attack our left flank, but found us too strong and he hastily withdrew under heavy fire. The ridge in I.6d still gave trouble, but as the south of the village was clear, a flanking movement was made and was entirely successful. Many of the enemy were found hurrying about the streets in DOMPIERRE and captured. The machine gunners on the ridge at I.6d were dealt with. Machine Gunners wearing red cross brassards were promptly shot. A total of about 50 prisoners were taken in this village, together with machine guns, the capture being completed by 1730 hours. The vanguard took a line of posts along the road east of DOMPIERRE, and later in the evening pushed over the line of the railway, the enemy being nowhere in sight. Battalion H.Q. was established in the house on the south side of the Church. The enemy had, early in the afternoon, blown up the railway bridge J.1d.1.4. and the river bridge and J.7a.3.5. The bridge at J.7a.4.4. was reported by civilians to be mined. Total prisoners taken during the day was about 80.

7th Nov. At about 0400 hours a representative of the R.E. came to examine the bridges. At 0815 hours the Battalion was ready to advance as part of the main body. The 21st Manchester Regt. being ordered to pass through the outpost line by 0800 hours. At about 1000 hours the Battalion, as part of the main body, passed along the road through J.1d, but the column was checked and no further progress made up to 1615 hours, when the order was given for the Battalion to withdraw and return to billets in DOMPIERRE. The Battalion was in billets at 1900 hours, H.Q. in the Mayor's house next to the Church.

8th Nov. At 1000 hours on the morning of the 8th November, the Battalion proceeded by march route through HUGEMONT - MARBAIX - MAROILLES - to billets in LANDRECIES arriving about 15 hours

APPENDIX IX

Secret. 20th Manchester Regiment. Ref. Map 1/40000. No.154.

1. The Bn. will move to Pommereuil today, 15th Nov. and take over billets from a Battalion of the 56th Bde.

2. Parade ready to move off at 10.30 hours. Order of march H.Q., Band, B.C.D.A and Transport.
The head of the column will be at the main road junction with this side street.

Intervals on the March. 100 yds. between Coys. and Coys. and Transport 100 yds. between every 8 vehicles.
Route.- Road junction G.16.d.4.4. - G.20.c.5.1. - L.29.a.4.3.

3. Blankets will be rolled in bundles of 10 and dumped at Q.M.Stores by 0730 hours. Officers valises, mess boxes, spare dixies, and band packs will be dumped at the same place not later than 0930 hours.
4. One motor lorry is allotted to this Unit for blankets and band packs. It will do one journey.

5. DRESS. Full marching order. Steel helmets to be worn. The helmets must be washed clean of all dirt.

6. The following billeting party will report to the Staff Capt at 1000 hours at Pommereuil Church. 2/Lt.J.T.Walley. C.Q.M.Sgts. Transport Representative. Parade at H.Q.Mess 0900 hours with cycles. The representatives must know billeting strengths.

Issued at 0400 hours. 13.11.19.

(Sgd) G.B.DEMPSEY.
Capt & Adjutant.

Copies to,-
1. C.O. & 2nd in C.
2. O.C. A Coy.
3. " B "
4. " C "
5. " D "
6. Q.M.
7. Transport Sgt.
8. Sgt. Mitchell.
9. H.Q.Mess.
11. File.
12. File.
13. War Diary.
14. War Diary.

SECRET   Copy No. 13

20th Bn. THE MANCHESTER REGIMENT.
ORDER No. 155.

Ref. Map
VALENCIENNES 1/100000.

1. The Battalion will move to QUIEVY tomorrow, the 29th November.

ROUTE. Road junction 3/4 mile West of Pau POMMEREUIL - MONTAY - NEUVILLY STATION - BRIASTRE - FARM 1/4 miles East of QUIEVY.

Battalion Starting Point :- 7th Brigade H.Q.
The head of the column will be at the starting point by 0814 hours.
Order of March. H.Q. Band, "A", "B", "C", "D" Transport.
Intervals to be maintained on the march :-
500 yards between Battalions, 100 yards between companies, 100 yards between companies and transport, 50 yards between every 12 vehicles.
Dress. Full marching order. Soft caps to be worn. Leather jerkins to be carried under the ground sheet under the flap of the pack.

2. Reveille 0600 hours. Breakfast 0700 hours. Sick Parade 0715
Blankets, rolled in bundles of 10, to be dumped at the Q.M. Stores by 0700 hours. Band packs will be dumped at the same time and place.
Officers kits, mess boxes, dixies and Orderly Room boxes to be at Q.M.Stores by 0800 hours.

3. The following billeting party will leave H.Q. at 0830 hours under the command of 2/Lt. J. Walley,-
(Cycles may be had from Orderly Room)
a/C.Q.M.Sergts. and X representatives from the Transport, and Q.M.Stores

4. The billets will be left thoroughly clean. Open latrines will be filled in. Billet boards etc. will be sent in to the Q.M.Stores by 0800 hours.
The Orderly Officer will obtain a certificate from the Area Commandant that billets vacated by this Battalion are in a clean and sanitary condition.

5. One motor lorry (doing two journeys) for the transport of blankets and stores will report to the Q.M. at 0700 hours.

6. The Signal Sergt. will circulate the correct time at 0730 hours.

Issued at 21 hours.
28.11.18.
                                                            B Dempsey
                                                        Captain & Adjutant.

Copy No. 1. H.Q. Mess
        2. B Mess
        3. O.C. A Coy.   8. T.O.
        4. O.C. B "   9. R.S.M.
        5. O.C. C "   10. Signal Sergt.
        6. O.C. D "   11. File.
        7. Q.M.   12. File.
                                 13. War Diary.
                                 14. War Diary.

APPENDIX V.

20th Battalion The Manchester Regiment.

Nominal Roll of Officers as on 30th November, 1918.

Colonel.
Lt.Colonel C.R.Pilkington C.M.G.................In hospital.
Major.
J.S.Gemmell M.C. ....With Battalion.
CAPTAINS.
F.Nicholls M.C. ....With Battalion.
A.G.N.Dixey M.C. ....With Battalion.
K.Rigby. ....On leave.
E.W.Sharpe. ....With Battalion.
P.Gillespie. ....With Battalion.
J.D.Luckhoff. ....With Battalion.

LIEUTENANTS.
G.F.S.Brownlow (A/Capt)..........................With Battalion.
H.S.Painter M.C. ....With Battalion.
E.W.Shaw. ....With Battalion.
E.H.Shackle M.C. ....With Battalion.
H.P.Vollmer. ....With Battalion.
R.O.Garside. ....On leave.

SECOND LIEUTENANTS. ....
D. Kitchen. ....With Battalion.
H.S.Latham. ....With Battalion.
J.Kilroe. ....With Battalion.
L.H.Spencer. ....On leave.
G.D.Ramsay. ....With Battalion.
J.T.Walley. ....With Battalion.
E.Crossley M.C. ....On leave.
J.Isherwood. ....With Battalion.
H.Branham. ....With Battalion.
P.Earle. ....With Battalion.
A.Drabble M.M. ....With Battalion.
W.N.Smith. ....With Battalion.
G.H.B.Hodges. ....With Battalion.
A.E.Owen. ....With Battalion.
D.Slack. ....With Battalion.
H.D.Telford. ....With Battalion.
E.Ingham M.M. ....With Battalion.
H.Sutton. ....With Battalion.
P.Darlington M.C. ....With Battalion.
S.W.Casson. ....Area Commdt. QUIEVY.
J.A.Feeney. ....With Battalion.

MEDICAL OFFICER.
Capt. P.E.Carroll. (R.A.M.C.).................With Battalion.
ADJUTANT.
Capt. G.B.Dempsey M.C.........................With Battalion.
QUARTERMASTER.
Capt. & Q.M. T.J.McKenna......................With Battalion.

1.12.18.

Major.
Cdg. 20th Bn. The Manchester Regt.

20th Bn. THE MANCHESTER REGIMENT.

Honours & Decorations awarded during Nov. 1918.

Capt. J.S.Gemmell M.C.	awarded	The Distinguished Service Order.
Capt. G.B.Dempsey M.C.	"	Bar to the Military Cross.
Capt. F. Nicholls,	"	The Military Cross,
A/Capt. G.W.L.Pritchard.	"	The Military Cross.

40388 L/c.	T.Betteley.	awarded	The Distinguished Conduct Medal.
17459 CSM.	H.Perry.	"	The Distinguished Conduct Medal.

The undermentioned awarded MILITARY MEDALS.

40333	Pte	H. Taylor	"D" Coy.	14783	Pte	S.Taylor	"D" Coy.
39666	"	F. Bradley	"A" "	14065	"	W.Summerscales	"C" "
44454	Cpl	A. Mills	"C" "	40208	L/c	T.Fothergill	"B" "
48966	Pte	A. Ellis	"B" "	44483	Pte	H.Shaw	"A" "
19110	Sgt	F. Evans	"A" "	40420	Sgt	W.Bradbury	"A" "
13501	Pte	C. Cassidy	"B" "	250487	Pte	W.Leigh	"C" "
1313	"	D. Doherty	"A" "	7688	"	C.Johnson	"B" "
17842	CQMS	H. Cadman	"D" "	200762	Sgt	J.Sherry	"D" "
17195	"	A.E.Phippen	"C" "	40206	Cpl	W.Barton	"B" "
54122	Pte	A.G.Hammond	"D" "	40519	"	A.Burgum	"B" "
44486	"	H. Waterhouse	"C" "				

1.12.18.

Major,
Cdg. 20th Bn. The Manchester Regt.

20th Bn. THE MANCHESTER REGIMENT.

Casualties during the Month of November, 1918.

OFFICERS

   2/Lt. J. Elder. Wounded 6.11.18.
   Lt.Col.C.R.Pilkington Sick 13.11.18.
              C.M.G.

OTHER RANKS.

   Killed in action...........4.
   Wounded...................24.
   Sick......................69.
   (Evacuations)

                            Major.
                  Cdg. 20th Bn. The Manchester Regt.

1.12.18.

20th Battalion the Manchester Regiment.

REINFORCEMENTS RECEIVED DURING MONTH OF NOVEMBER, 1918.

OFFICERS.

Date of arrival.

Capt. J.D.Luckhoff	11.11.18.
" K.Rigby	14.11.18.
Lieut. R.O.Garside	14.11.18.
2/Lt. H.Sutton	do
" P.Darlington M.C	16.11.18.
" A.Drabble M.M.	17.11.18.
" W.N.Smith	do
" A.E.Owen	do
" D.Slack	do
" S.W.Casson	do
Capt. P.Gillespie	do
" E.W.Sharpe	20.11.18.
2/Lt. P.Earle	30.11.18.
" G.H.B.Hodges	do
" H.D.Telford	do
" J.A.Feeney	do
" E.Ingham M.M	4.11.18.

Other Ranks.

96	Other Ranks	joined	Battalion	1.11.18.
87	"	"	"	"	6.11.18.
5	"	"	"	"	2.11.18.
3	"	"	"	"	3.11.18.
7	"	"	"	"	13.11.18.
2	"	"	"	"	15.11.18.
8	"	"	"	"	21.11.18.
6	"	"	"	"	26.11.18.
4	"	"	"	"	27.11.18.
9	"	"	"	"	30.11.18.

1.12.18.

[signature] Major,
Cdg. 20th Bn. The Manchester Regt.

Secret.

Vol 38

20th BATTALION,
THE MANCHESTER
REGIMENT
No. 7212
Date 5-1-19

War Diary
— of —

20th Battalion The Manchester Regiment.

From 1st December, 1918   To 31st December, 1918.

Volume XXXVIII

A.C. Curry   Lieut. Colonel.
Cdg. 20th Battn The Manchester Regt.

Army Form C. 2118.

WAR DIARY
INTELLIGENCE SUMMARY.
(Erase heading not required.)

Volume XXVII Sheet 1
December 1918

Place	Date	Hour	Summary of Events and Information	Remarks and references to Appendices
QUIEVY.	1st		Church Parade in morning. Weather fine.	
	2nd–3rd		Battalion carried out salvage work in vicinity of QUIEVY. Examination of miners' tunnages to Croisilles' Enemy Reserve completed.	
Sheet 57B 1/40,000	4th		His Majesty the King visited the village at 1340 hours. No salvage work on training carried out.	
	5th–6th		Salvage work continued in vicinity of village. Weather unsettled. Rain at intervals on wet day.	
	8th		Church Parade in morning.	
	9th		Battalion moved at 1030 hours via BEVILLERS to BIEVILLERS arriving about 1200 hours. Billets unsettled.	
FONTAINE au PIRE.			in FONTAINE au PIRE arriving about 1200 hours. Billets on the whole - good.	
	10th–14th		Two Companies on salvage work on rear area and two Companies training. Weather unsettled.	
	15th		Church Parade in morning.	
	16th		Battalion marched to Divnl Baths AVESNES les AUBERT.	

WAR DIARY or INTELLIGENCE SUMMARY

Army Form C. 2118.

Sheet II

December 1918.

Place	Date	Hour	Summary of Events and Information	Remarks and references to Appendices
FONTAINE au PIRE	17th		Two Companies continued Salvage work. Remainder of Battⁿ training and Bathing. Lieut Col A.C. CROYDON MC DCM arrived from Base and took Command.	
Sheet 57B 1/40000	18th-21st		Battalion continued salvage of work. Weather unsettled	
	22nd		Church Parade in morning	
	23rd		Battalion continued Salvage operations	
	24th } 25th } 26th }		Observed as holidays. No salvage. Training or Educational work carried out	
	27th } 28th }		Battalion on Salvage work. Weather very wet.	
	29th		Church parades in morning. Weather wet.	
	30th		Battalion on Salvage work. Weather unsettled	
	31st		Battalion at Baths at QUIEVY.	

A.C. Croyden Lieut Col
Commanding Battalion Manchester Regiment

20th Service Battalion Manchester Regiment.

57B 1/40,000
Sheet 57B 1/40,000

Area held by Bn outlined in Red. D.

SECRET.   Copy No. 14

                20th Bn. THE MANCHESTER REGIMENT.
                        ORDER No. 156.

Ref. Maps VALENCIENNES 1/100000.
          57B   1/40000.

1. The Battalion will move tomorrow the 9th Dec. to BEAUVOIS.
   Route. BEVILLERS - BEAUVOIS.

2. Parade in the PLACE des ARMES in column of route ready to move
   off at 10.30 hours.
   Order of March. H.Q. Band, "B" Coy. "C" Coy. "D" Coy. "A" Coy.
   Transport.
   Dress. Full marching order with soft caps.
   Intervals. 100 yards between Companies.
              100   "   "   Transport and the rear of "A" Coy.
               50   "   "   each group of 12 vehicles.

3. Reveille 07.00 hours. Breakfast 07.30 hours. Sick Parade 08.00 hours.
   Blankets (rolled in bundles of 10) to be at the Q.M.Stores by 08.30 hrs.
   Officers kits, mess boxes, spare dixies)
   band packs etc. Packs of N.C.Os and   ) to be at the Q.M.Stores
   men on Presentation Parade, Orderly   )   09.00 hours.
   Room boxes etc.   )

4. The advance party, as detailed for today, will leave "B" Mess at
   08.30 hours.

5. Platoon and Coy. billet boards will be carried in Company Lewis
   Gun Limbers.

6. Billets and billet surroundings will be left thoroughly clean.
   Open latrines will be filled in.
   The Orderly Officer will obtain from the Town Major, a certificate
   to the effect that billets have been left in a clean and sanitary
   condition.
                                                  G B Dempsey
   Issued at 1430 hours.   Capt. & Adjutant.
   8.12.18.   20th Manchester Regiment.

   Copy No. 1. H.Q. 7th Bde.   Copy No. 9. R.S.M.
        2.   H.Q.Mess.   10. a/R.Q.M.S.
        3.   "B" Mess.   11. Transport Officer.
        4.   O.C. "A" Coy.   12. File.
        5.   "   "B" "   13. War Diary.
        6.   "   "C" "   14. "   "
        7.   "   "D" "

SECRET.   Copy No. 12

20th Bn. THE MANCHESTER REGIMENT.
ORDER No. 167.

Ref. Map VALENCIENNES 1/100000.

1. The Battalion will move tomorrow 1.1.19 to BRIASTRE.
Route, BEAUVOIS - BEVILLERS - QUIEVY. Farm, Point 119 - BRIASTRE.
Battalion starting point at D Coy. Officers Mess.
Order of March, H.Q. - Band, D, A, B, C, Companies, Transport,
The head of the column will pass the starting point at 08.30 hours -
Dress - Full marching order with soft caps.

INTERVALS. 100 yds. between Coys.
          100 "   "   Transport and rear of "C" Coy.
          50   "   "   each group of 12 vehicles.

2. Reveille 06.30 hours, Breakfast 07.00 hours. Sick Parade 08.00 hrs.
Blankets (rolled in bundles of 10) to be dumped at the "C" Coy.
Billet (opposite Orderly Room) by 08.00 hours.
Officers kits, mess boxes, spare dixies, Orderly Room boxes to be
at respective Coy. H.Q. by 08.00 hours ready for collection.
The Q.M. will arrange to collect.
Band Packs to be at Q.Ms. Stores by 08.00 hours.
Os.C. Companies to detail two men as loading party for blankets etc.

3. The following billeting party will leave Orderly Room at 08.30
hours. Capt. SHARPE, Coy. Q.M.Sergts, Sgt. STOTT and representatives
from Transport and Q.Ms. Stores. They will report to Area Commdt.
BRIASTRE on arrival there. Each C.Q.M.Sergt. and sub unit
representative must know his billeting strength. Cycles can be
obtained from Orderly Room.

4. Platoon and Company Billet Boards will be carried on Coy. L.G.
Limbers.

5. Billets and billet surroundings will be left thoroughly clean.
Latrines will be filled in. Latrine seats, screens &c. will be
collected and dumped in rear of "B" Company billet.
O.C. "B" Company will detail 1 N.C.O. and 3 men to remain on
guard over this dump, pending its removal to new billets.
The Orderly Officer will obtain from the Town Major a certificate
that billets have been left in a clean and sanitary condition.

Issued at 2045 hours.   J.M.Whalley 2/Lt.A/Adjutant,
31.12.18.   20 Bn. THE MANCHESTER REGT.

        Copy No. 1. H.Q.Mess   Copy No. 8. Q.M.
              2. "B" "   9. T.O.
              3. O.C. "A" Coy.   10. File.
              4.   "B" "   11. War Diary.
              5.   "C" "   12. War Diary.
              6.   "D" "
              7.   R.S.M.

20th Bn. THE MANCHESTER REGIMENT.

NOMINAL ROLL OF OFFICERS AS ON 31.12.18.

Colonel.
Lt.Col. A.C.Croydon, M.C. D.C.M............With Battalion.
Major.
Major J.S.Gemmell, D.S.O. M.C..............With Battalion.
CAPTAINS.
P.Gillespie................................With Battalion.
J.D.Luckhoff...............................With Battalion.
E.W.Sharpe.................................With Battalion.
F.Nicholls, D.S.O. M.C.....................On leave.
A.G.N.Dixey, M.C...........................On leave.

LIEUTENANTS.
K.Rigby (A/Capt)...........................With Battalion.
H.S.Painter, M.C...........................With Battalion.
E.H.Shackle, M.C...........................With Battalion.
E.W.Shaw...................................With Battalion.
R.O.Garside................................On leave.
G.F.S.Brownlow.............................On leave.
H.P.Vollmer................................On leave.

SECOND LIEUTENANTS.
D.Kitchen, M.C. (A/Capt)...................With Battalion.
J.Isherwood, M.C. (A/Capt).................With Battalion.
P.Earle....................................With Battalion.
H.Branham, M.C.............................With Battalion.
D.Slack....................................With Battalion.
H.S.Latham.................................With Battalion.
W.N.Smith..................................With Battalion.
H.Sutton...................................With Battalion.
L.H.Spencer................................With Battalion.
E.Crossley, M.C............................With Battalion.
H.D.Telford................................With Battalion.
A.Drabble, M.M.............................With Battalion.
A.E.Owen...................................With Battalion.
S.R.Pike...................................With Battalion.
E.Ingham, M.M..............................With Battalion.
J.Kilroe...................................With Battalion.
J.A.Feeney.................................With Battalion.
P.Darlington, M.C..........................With Battalion.
G.H.B.Hodges...............................With Battalion.
H.Willis...................................With Battalion.
R.L.Hardisty...............................With Battalion.
K.B.Lodge..................................With Battalion.
T.Garratt..................................With Battalion.
S.W.Casson.................................Area Commdt. QUIEVY.
G.D.Ramsay.................................Chemical Course, DOULLENS.

ASSISTANT ADJUTANT.
2/Lt. J.T.Walley......   *With Battalion*
MEDICAL OFFICER.
Capt. P.E.Carroll. (R.A.M.C.)..............With Battalion.

ADJUTANT.
Captain G.B.Dempsey, M.C...................On leave.

QUARTERMASTER.
Capt. & Q.M.T.J.McKenna....................With Battalion.

3.1.19.

A.C.Croydon, Lieut.Colonel.
Cdg.20th Bn.THE MANCHESTER REGT.

20th Bn. THE MANCHESTER REGIMENT.

Honours & Decorations awarded during the month of Dec. 1918.

Capt. F. Nicholls, M.C.	awarded	The Distinguished Service Order.
2/Lt (A/Capt) J.Isherwood	"	The Military Cross.
" " D.Kitchen	"	ditto.
2/Lt. H. Branham.	"	ditto.
" J. Elder.	"	ditto.
20552 L/c J.E.Crompton	"	The Distinguished Conduct Medal. (Killed in Action 6.11.18).

3.1.19.

A.E.Cusworth   Lt.Colonel,
Cdg. 20th Bn. THE MANCHESTER REGT.

20th Bn. THE MANCHESTER REGIMENT.

REINFORCEMENTS RECEIVED DURING THE MONTH OF DECEMBER, 1918.

OFFICERS.

		Date of arrival.
Lt.Colonel	A.C.Croydon, M.C. D.C.M.	17.12.18.
2/Lt.	R.K.Hardisty	2.12.18.
"	T.Garratt	5.12.18.
"	S.R.Pike	2.12.18.
"	H.Williss	2.12.18.
"	K.E.Lodge	13.12.18.

OTHER RANKS.

54 O.R. received from BASE.

3.1.19.

A.C.Croydon, Lt.Colonel,
Cdg. 20th Bn./THE MANCHESTER REGT.

SECRET.

> 20th BATTALION,
> THE MANCHESTER
> REGIMENT.
>
> No.............
> Date............

WAR   DIARY

of

20th Battalion THE MANCHESTER REGIMENT

From, 1st January, 1919..To, 31st January, 1919.

Volume XXXIX

A C Croydon Lieut. Colonel,
Cdg. 20th Bn. The Manchester Regt.

Army Form C. 2118.

WAR DIARY
or
INTELLIGENCE SUMMARY.
(Erase heading not required.)

Sheet 1

VOL XXIX   January 1919

Place	Date	Hour	Summary of Events and Information	Remarks and references to Appendices
FRANCE	1st		Battalion moved from FONTAINE au PIRE at 1000 hours via BEAUVOIS-	Appx I
VALENCIENNES		1000	BEVILLERS- QUIEVY to BRIASTRE arriving about 1300 hours. Billet's in very bad condition. H.Q. established in house at crossroads near Church.	pass
			Weather unsettled.	
BRIASTRE	2nd		No parade. Motor lorries provided to convey Battalion to CAMBRAI to Divisional entertainment. Weather unsettled.	pass
	3rd		Battalion moved at 0930 hours via SOLESMES- BEAUVAIN- VENDEGIES- to POIX du NORD arriving about 1300 hours. Billets exceptionally good.	Appx II
POIX du NORD			Weather fine.	pass
	4th		Day spent in cleaning up billets & their surroundings.	pass
Start 5.2.6	5th		Weather fine.	pass
Hours-	6th		Usual Church Parade services	pass
	7th to	10h	Battalion practiced Ceremonial Drill.	pass
	9th to	10h	Battalion worked on Salvage area.	pass
	11th		Ceremonial Drill	pass
	12th		Usual Church Parades.	pass

WAR DIARY
INTELLIGENCE SUMMARY.
(Erase heading not required.)

Army Form C. 2118.

Place	Date	Hour	Summary of Events and Information	Remarks and references to Appendices
POIX DU NORD.	13th		Battalion worked on Salvage Area.	D.R.
	14th/15th		Ceremonial Drill	D.R.
	19th		Usual Church Parades.	D.R.
	20		Salvage on new area	
	21		"	A.B.S.
	22		A + B. C + D bathing	
	23		Ceremonial Drill	
	24		A + B Salvage - C + D Drill	
	25		C + D Salvage - A + B - Route March	
	26		Church Parade	A.B.S.
	27		Baths for A + B. C + D Clearing own farm lands	
	28		Baths for C + D Ceremonial	
	29		Presented with Colours.	N.T.
	30.		Route March	
	31		Route March	

A.C. Crosydon
Lieut Colonel Comm.
10th Service Battalion Worcs.

SECRET.

20th Bn. The Manchester Regiment
ORDER No. 158.

Copy No- 12

Ref. Map :-
VALENCIENNES, 1/100,000.

1. The Battalion will move tomorrow 3.1.19. to POIX du NORD, Route :- SOLESMES - BEAURAIN - VENDEGIES - POIX du NORD. Order of March, H.Q., Band, A, B, C, D, Coys, Transport. Starting point, Factory on SOLESMES road. Coys will be in position ready to move off at 0930 hours. Dress :- Full Marching Order, with soft caps. The usual intervals will be maintained, i.e. 100 yards between Coys - 100 yards between rear of "D" Coy and Transport. 50 yards between each group of 12 vehicles.

2. Reveille 0630 hours, Breakfast 0700 hours, Sick Parade 0800 hours. Blankets (rolled in bundles of 10) to be dumped under cover at the respective Coy H.Q. by 0800 hours ready for collection by the Quartermaster. Officers Kits, Mess Boxes, Spare Dixies, Orderly Room Boxes to be at respective Coy H.Q. by 0800 hours, ready for collection by the Quartermaster. Band Packs to be at Q.M. Stores by 0800 hours. O.C.Coys will each detail two men as loading party for blankets etc.-

3. Billets and surroundings will be left thoroughly clean and open latrines filled in. Billeting Certificates will be rendered and 2nd Lieut. A. DRAPER., will obtain certificate of cleanliness from Area Commandant.-

Issued at 1915 hours.
2.1.19.

Wadley
2nd Lieut. A/Adjutant.

Copy No. 1.	H.Q. Mess.	Copy No. 7.	R.S.M.
2.	"B" Mess.	8.	Q.M.
3.	O.C. "A" Coy.	9.	T.O.
4.	.. "B" ..	10.	File.
5.	.. "C" ..	11.	War Diary.
6.	.. "D" ..	12.	do.

20th Battalion The Manchester Regiment.

NOMINAL ROLL OF OFFICERS AS ON 31ST JANUARY, 1919.

                                                                Location.

COLONEL.
- Lt.COL.A.C.Croydon, MC. DCM. ....With Battalion.
  (5th West Yorks).

MAJORS.
- J.S.Gemmell, DSO. MC. ....On Leave.

CAPTAINS.
- J.D.Luckhoff (General List) ....On Leave.
- F.Nicholls, DSO. MC. ....On Leave.
- A.G.N.Dixey, MC. ....On Leave.
- E.W.Sharpe. (D.of L.Y.)....................With Battalion.

LIEUTENANTS.
- G.F.S.Brownlow (A/Capt)....................With Battalion.
- H.S.Painter, MC. ....In Hospital.
- E.W.Shaw.. ....With Battalion.
- E.H.Shackle, MC. ....In Hospital.
- H.P.Vollmer. ....On Leave.

SECOND LIEUTENANTS.
- D.Kitchen, MC. (A/Capt)....................On Conducting Duty.
- P.Earle. ....With Battalion.
- P.Darlington, MC. ....On Leave.
- H.Branham, MC. ....On Conducting Duty.
- D.Slack. ....With Battalion.
- H.S.Latham. ....In Hospital.
- W.N.Smith. ....On Conducting Duty.
- H.Sutton,(D. of L.Y.) ....In Hospital.
- L.H.Spencer. ....With Battalion.
- E.Crossley, MC. .... do.
- H.D.Telford. .... do.
- A.Drabble, MM. .... do.
- A.E.Owen. .... do.
- S.R.Pike. ....On Leave.
- J.Kilroe. ....On Conducting Duty.
- J.A.Feeney. ....Army Burial H.Q.
- G.H.B.Hodges. ....With Battalion.
- R.L.Hardisty. .... do.
- K.B.Lodge. (D. of L.Y.)..................... do.
- T.Garratt. .... do.
- S.W.Casson. ....Area Commdt., QUIEVY.
- G.D.Ramsay. ....Chemical Course, DOULLENS.
- C.Parker. ....With Battalion.
- J.T.Walley, MC. ....On Conducting Duty.

ADJUTANT.
- Captain G.B.Dempsey, MC....................With Battalion.

MEDICAL OFFICER.
- Captain P.E.Carroll (R.A.M.C.)............. do.

A/QUARTERMASTER.
- Sec.Lieut.E.Ingham, MM..................... do.

....

3.2.19.   ACCroyden   Lieut.Colonel.
                Cdg.20th Battn.The Manchester Regiment.

20th Battalion The Manchester Regiment.

CASUALTIES DURING THE MONTH OF JANUARY, 1919.

Officers.
```
Captain P.Gillespie. ...............To U.K. for Demobilization
                                           21.1.19.
Sec.Lt.(A/Capt)Isherwood, MC.......To U.K. for Demobilization
                                           7.1.19.
Sec.Lieut.H.Willis.................To U.K. for Demobilization
                                           13.1.19.
Capt.T.J.McKenna.(Quartermaster)...To U.K. (Sick) 13.1.19.
Lieut.(A/Capt)K.Rigby..............To U.K. (Sick) 13.1.19.
       (Duke of Lancs.Yeo)
Lieut.R.O.Garside..................Struck off strength in U.K.
                                        (Med.Board) 3.1.19.
```

Other Ranks.

Number of Other Ranks proceeded to U.K. for Demobilization :-

155.

....

3.2.19.   Commdg.20th Battn.The Manchester Regiment.   Lieut.Colonel.

20th Battalion The Manchester Regiment.
-:-:-:-:-:-:-:-:-:-:-:-:-:-:-:-:-:-:-

R E I N F O R C E M E N T S

Received during the Month of JANUARY, 1919.
-:-:-:-:-:-:-:-:-:-:-

Officers:-

Sec.Lieut.CMParker........Arrivedefrom Base...4.1.19.

Other Ranks:-

Number of Other Ranks (Casuals) received from Base:- 35.

3.2.19.

Lieut.Colonel
Cdg.20th Bn.The Manchester Regiment.

20th Battalion The Manchester Regiment.

HONOURS AND DECORATIONS AWARDED DURING THE MONTH OF JANUARY, 1919.

<u>Third</u>- Supplement to the London Gazette dated 31.12.18.

Sec.Lieut.J.T.Walley.   Awarded the MILITARY CROSS.

17037 RQMS Campbell, R.A. Awarded the MERITORIOUS SERVICE MEDAL.
40521 A/Cpl.Bell,   W.   do.   do.   do.
40468 L/C. Nickson, F.   do.   do.   do.

<u>Second Supplement to London Gazette dated 3.1.19</u>:-

MENTIONED in General F.R.Earl of CAVAN'S DESPATCHES d/- 26.10.18:-
<u>South Staffordshire Regt</u>.
    Lt.Col.C.S.Burt. D.S.O. 1st Bn. att. 20th Manchr.R.
<u>Manchester Regt</u>.
    Lieut.T.M.Newin.
    Sec.Lieut.L.J.Poynter.
    Sec.Lieut.E.M.Wright.
    17280 L/C. J.Allen
    54136 Cpl.H.O.Churchill-Carter.
    19362 L/Sgt.W.Darbyshire.
    54120 Pte.G.H.Goodale.
    33844 Pte.F.Page.
    17524 Pte.W.T.Worland, DCM.

3.2.19.   Lieut.Colonel.
                          Commdg.20th Battn.The Manchester Regt.

SECRET.

WAR DIARY
of

20th Battalion THE MANCHESTER REGIMENT

From, 1st February, 1919....To, 28th February, 1919.

Volume XL.

                                                                    Lieut. Colonel.
                                            Cdg. 20th Bn. THE MANCHESTER REGIMENT.

Army Form C. 2118.

WAR DIARY
or
INTELLIGENCE SUMMARY.
(Erase heading not required.)

Sheet 1.

VOLUME XL February 1919

Place	Date	Hour	Summary of Events and Information	Remarks and references to Appendices
POIX DU NORD	Feb 1st		Route March	
	2		Church Parade	
Sheet 57B	3		B. C & D Batting "A" at disposal of Coy. Cmdr.	RM
Mucco	4		Route March	
	5		Route March	
	6		Organized wood parties to Mormal Forest	RM
	7		Clearing roads of snow (In Bn Area)	RM
	8		do	RM
	9		Church Parade	RM
	10		Wood parties to Mormal forest	RM
	11		Bathing	RM
	12		Fencing Cemetries	RM
	13		— do —	RM
	14		— do —	RM
	15		Battalion at work on salvage areas, removing dumps &c	RM
	16		Church Parades	RM

WAR DIARY
or
INTELLIGENCE SUMMARY.
(Erase heading not required.)

Army Form C. 2118.

Sheet 2.

VOL XL February 1919

Place	Date	Hour	Summary of Events and Information	Remarks and references to Appendices
POIX au NORD	Feby. 17th	18.00	Battalion on Salvagework, Collection of Stores &c preparatory to move.	See.
	19th		Battalion moved at 0900 hours from POIX du NORD via VENDEGIES-	
Shed 6"B. 1400000			BEAURAIN-SOLESMES- to ST. VAAST arriving at latter place about 1400 hours.	See. I
ST. VAAST.	20th		March continued at 1000 hours from ST VAAST to CAMBRAI. Destination reached by 1330 hours. Battalion H.Q. established at Rielle No. 26. Rue du Petit Seminaire.	App x See.
CAMBRAI	21st		Parade hours devoted to Foot Inspections, & general cleaning up of Rifles, equipment &c.	See.
	22nd		Parade hours devoted to cleaning up Billets &c.	See.
	23rd		Church Parades.	See.
	24th		Parade hours devoted to Physical Training, Arms & Guard Mounting drill, and reconnaisance of new Salvage area	See.
	25th		Salvage work on new area, sorting and classifying	See.
	26th		dumps &c.	See.

Army Form C. 2118.

WAR DIARY
or
INTELLIGENCE SUMMARY.
(Erase heading not required.)

Sheet 3

Vol XL February 1919.

Place	Date	Hour	Summary of Events and Information	Remarks and references to Appendices
CAMBRAI. Sheet 57.B. 1/40.0.10.	Feb. 27th		Divisional Baths in Rue du Belfort allotted to the Battalion from	249
	28th	0945 to 1700 hours.		

A.C. Cherington Lieutenant Colonel Commanding
80th. Service Battalion Manchester Regiment

SECRET.   20th BN. THE MANCHESTER REGIMENT   Copy No. 15

ORDER No. 159.

Ref. Map :- VALENCIENNES, 1/100,000.   18.2.19.

1. The Battalion will move by march route to CAMBRAI on the 19th and 20th February, staging the night 19/20th February at ST. VAAST.

2. The following intervals will be maintained on the march on each day:-
   100 yards between Companies.
   100 yards between the rear of the last Coy and the head of the Transport.
   50 yards between each group of vehicles.

3. Watches will be synchronised each morning at 0700 hours. Dress for each days march :- Full marching order with soft caps.

4. Move for the 19th February from POIX DU NORD Destination ST. VAAST. Route. VENDEGIES - BEAURAIN - SOLESMES. Starting Point, La Filature, the westernmost house in POIX DU NORD (past "D" Coy mess). Time 0900 hours. Order of March :- H.Q.(under 2/Lt. WALLEY,M.C.), No.1 Coy, No.2 Coy, Transport. The column will be in position ready to move by 0900 hours. Reveille. 0600 hours, Breakfast. 0630 hours, Sick Parade. 0700 hours.

   Blankets, rolled tightly in bundles of ten, Officers kits and mess boxes etc, will be loaded on the Village Green direct into the wagons. All articles to be loaded not later than 0800 hours. "A" Coy will supply loading party of 1 Officer, 2 N.C.Os and 12 men to commence loading at 0700 hours.

5. Move for the 20th February from ST. VAAST. Destination, CAMBRAI.   Route, direct road to CAMBRAI. Starting Point - ST. VAAST Church.   Time, 1000 hours. Order of March - H.Q.(under 2/Lt. WALLEY,M.C.), No.1 Coy, No.2 Coy, Transport. The column will be in position ready to move by 1000 hours. Reveille, 0630 hours. Breakfast, 0700 hours. Sick Parade, 0730 hours.
   Blankets, tightly rolled in bundles of ten, Officers kits and mess boxes will be loaded at the Q.M.Stores not later than 0900 hours. No.2 Coy will supply a loading party of 1 Officer 2 N.C.Os and 12 men to commence loading at 0800 hours.

6. O.C.Coys and sub units will ensure by personal inspection that :-
   a/ Billets are left scrupulously clean each day.
   b/ Men are properly dressed for the march, that no unauthorised articles are slung from the equipment, and rags are not tied on the muzzles of rifles.

7. The Q.M. will detail the 2 motor lorries running to CAMBRAI on the 19th to report at No.18, Rue de la Porte Robert (Bde. H.Q) where a guide detailed by Lieut. P.DARLINGTON,M.C., will meet them and guide them to the Q.M.Stores in CAMBRAI.
   The special guard on the Q.M.Stores will travel on the second lorry, if all stores are cleared, with the A/R.Q.M.Sgt. The first lorry will be accompanied by Sergt. ROOD and an unloading party of 4 men certified by the M.O. as unfit to march. This party will remain as guard over stores at CAMBRAI until the arrival of the Battalion. No other persons will travel on the motor lorries.

Issued at 1500 hours
18.2.19.
                                                    G.B.Dempsey
                                                  Captain & Adjutant.

Copy No. 1, C.O.
        2, 2/Lt. WALLEY,M.C.   Copy No.10, O.C."D" Coy.
        3, Medical Officer.   11, R.S.M.
        4, Transport Officer.   12, A/R.Q.M.S.
        5, Quartermaster.   13, Sgt. ROOD.
        6, Capt. LUCKHOFF.   14, File.
        7, O.C. "A" Coy.   15, War Diary.
        8, "   "B" "   16,
        9, "   "C" "

20th Bn. The Manchester Regiment.

NOMINAL ROLL OF OFFICERS AS ON 28th FEBRUARY, 1919

Location.

COLONEL.
    Lt. Col. A.C.Croydon, M.C., DCM................ With Battalion.
        (5th West Yorks).

MAJORS.

CAPTAINS.
    J.D.Luckhoff, (General List)................ With Battalion.
    A.G.N.Dixey, M.C. .... On Leave.
% E.W.Sharpe. (D.of L.Y)....................... With Battalion.
    G.F.S.Brownlow. .... - do.-

LIEUTENANTS
    H.S.Painter, M.C. .... In Hospital.
    E.W.Shaw. .... With Battalion.
    E.H.Shackle, M.C. .... - do -
    P.Earle. .... - do -
    P.Darlington, M.C. .... - do -

SECOND LIEUTENANTS.
    D.Kitchen, M.C. (A/Capt).................... With Battalion.
    H.Branham, M.C. .... - do -
    D.Slack. .... Conducting Duty.
    H.S.Latham. .... In Hospital.
    W.N.Smith. .... ~~With Battalion.~~ Cond:Duty.
    L.H.Spencer. .... ~~- do -~~ With Battn.
    E.Crossley, M.C. .... - do -
    H.D.Telford. .... - do -
    A.Drabble, M.M. .... Conducting Duty.
    A.E.Owen. .... With Battalion.
    S.R.Pike. .... - do -
    J.Kilroe. .... - do -
    J.A.Feeney. .... Army Burials, MEAULTE.
    G.H.B.Hodges. .... With Battalion.
    R.L.Hardisty. .... - do -
    K.E.Lodge. (D.of L.Y)........................ Conducting Duty (Horses)
    T.Garratt. .... 25th M.T.Coy. ST.AUBERT.
    S.W.Casson. .... With Battalion.
    G.D.Ramsay. .... Conducting Duty.
    J.T.Walley, M.C. .... With Battalion.

ADJUTANT.
    Captain G.B.Dempsey (M.C).................... With Battalion.

MEDICAL OFFICER.
    Captain P.E.Carroll (R.A.M.C)................ With Battalion.

A/QUARTERMASTER.
% Captain E.W.Sharpe........................... With Battalion.

:..

2.3.19.
                      A.C.Croydon Lieut. Colonel,
                      Cdg. 20th Bn. The Manchester Regiment.

20th Bn. THE MANCHESTER REGIMENT.

CASUALTIES DURING THE MONTH OF FEBRUARY, 1919.

OFFICERS.

Lieut.	H.P. VOLLMER.	- Demobilised whilst on Leave U.K.	3.1.19.
2/Lieut.	C. PARKER	- To U.K. for Demobilisation.	8.2.19.
2/Lieut.	E. INGHAM. M.M.	- To U.K. REGULAR OFFICER.	8.2.19.
MAJOR	J.S. GEMMELL, D.S.O. M.C.	- On Leave pending Demobilisation struck off	4.2.19.
Captain	F. NICHOLLS, D.S.O. M.C.	- DO -	6.1.19.
2/Lieut.	H. SUTTON.	To U.K. for Demobilisation.	24.2.19.

OTHER RANKS.

NUMBER OF OTHER RANKS PROCEEDED TO U.K. FOR

       DEMOBILISATION :- 236.

    TO U.K. RE-ENLISTED :- 16.

A C Croydon Lieut. Colonel.
Cdg. 20th Bn. THE MANCHESTER REGIMENT.

20th Bn. THE MANCHESTER REGIMENT.

REINFORCEMENTS

RECEIVED DURING THE MONTH OF FEBRUARY. 1919.

OFFICERS.

— NIL —

OTHER RANKS.

NUMBER OF OTHER RANKS (CASUALS) RECEIVED FROM BASE:— 9.

..........................Lieut. Colonel.
Cdg. 20th Bn. THE MANCHESTER REGIMENT.

20th Bn. THE MANCHESTER REGIMENT.

HONOURS AND DECORATIONS AWARDED DURING THE MONTH OF FEBRUARY, 1919.

AWARDED THE MILITARY MEDAL BY CORPS COMMANDER.

No. 40092 Pte. J. KIDDER.
No. 40514 Pte. T. MCLYNN.
No. 44482 Pte. A. MORRIS.
No. 34466 Pte. A. AUSTIN.

[signature] Lieut. Colonel.
Cdg. 20th Bn. THE MANCHESTER REGIMENT.

SECRET.

WAR   DIARY
of
20th Battalion THE MANCHESTER REGIMENT

From, 1st March, 1919....... To, 31st March, 1919.

VOLUME...... XL1

A C Curuydon Lieut. Colonel,
Cdg. 20th Bn. The Manchester Regiment.

WAR DIARY
or
INTELLIGENCE SUMMARY.

Army Form C. 2118.

(Erase heading not required.)

Place	Date	Hour	Summary of Events and Information	Remarks and references to Appendices
	MARCH			
CAMBRAI	1		Drill - Physical training - Squad and Company Drill.	S.K.
	2		Church Parades - Section fire.	S.K.
	3		Training - Squad Drill and Marching Drill - Company Drill	S.K.
	4		Training - as for March 3rd. - rifle and coy.	S.K.
	5		Salvage work. weaker fire	S.K.
	6		Baths for No 1 Coy: No 2 Coy Employed on Salvage.	S.K.
	7		Salvage for No 1 Coy. Baths for No 2 Coy	S.K.
	8		Royal Educational classes carry out training	S.K.
	9		Church Parades - weaker fire	S.K.
	10		Training as for March 3rd	S.K.
	11		Training on Parade Ground - Guard mounting - Communication Drill	S.K.
	12		Salvage. Weaker sight and fire.	S.K.
	13		Salvage for No 1 Coy Training for No 2	S.K.
	14		Training as per issued Programme.	S.K.
	15		Training further Educational classes: other clean up billets etc	S.K.
	16		Church Parades - Slight rain	S.K.

Army Form C. 2118.

WAR DIARY
or
INTELLIGENCE SUMMARY.
(Erase heading not required.)

Instructions regarding War Diaries and Intelligence Summaries are contained in F. S. Regs., Part II, and the Staff Manual respectively. Title pages will be prepared in manuscript.

Place	Date	Hour	Summary of Events and Information	Remarks and references to Appendices
CAMBRAI	MARCH 17.		Baths for No 2 Coy. Training for No 1.	J.K.
	18.		Baths for No 1 Coy. Training for No. 2.	J.K.
	19.		Training - Lecture to officers of Army of Occupation by Adjutant. Raining	J.K.
	20.		Rain all day. Routine.	J.K.
	21.		Paid to 20th.	J.K.
	22.		Training for men attending shows during off days. Cleaning up billets.	J.K.
	23.		Church Parades. Slight Rain	J.K.
	24.		Baths for No 1 Coy. Training for No 2. Fine but very cold.	J.K.
	25.		Baths for No 2 Coy. Training for No 1. Rain & sleet.	J.K.
	26.		Army of Occupation departed for the Rhine - Fine but very cold.	J.K.
	27.		Cadre only remain - All men are employed	J.K.
	28.		Very cold weather.	J.K.
	29.		Paid to 27th. Snow Show.	J.K.
	30.			
	31.			

A. Curry Major
Lieutenant Colonel Commanding
20th. Service Battalion Manchester Regiment.

20th Bn. The Manchester Regiment.

NOMINAL ROLL OF OFFICERS AS ON 31st MARCH, 1919.

COLONEL.
Lieut. Colonel A.C.Croydon, M.C.,D.C.M. ...... With Battalion.

LIEUTENANTS.
D.Kitchen, M.C. (A/Capt) .... With Battalion.
H.S.Painter,M.C. .... In Hospital.

SECOND LIEUTENANTS.
R.L.Hardisty .... With Battalion.
L.H.Spencer .... In Hospital.
S.W.Casson .... On Conductg. Duty.
J.A.Feeney .... With Army Burials, MEAULTE.

ADJUTANT.
Captain G.B.Dempsey, M.C. .... With B attalion.

A/QUARTERMASTER.
Captain E.W.Sharpe. (Duke Lancs. Yeomy).... With Battalion.

A.C.Croydon Lieut. Colonel,
Cdg. 20th Bn. The Manchester Regiment.

31-3-19-

20th Bn. The Manchester Regiment.

REINFORCEMENTS
RECEIVED DURING THE MONTH OF MARCH, 1919.

OFFICERS.

-- N I L --

OTHER RANKS.

NUMBER OF OTHER RANKS (CASUALS) RECEIVED FROM BASE............ 8.

ACCuryden Lieut. Colonel,
Cdg. 20th Bn. The Manchester Regiment.

31-3-19.

20th Bn. The Manchester Regiment.

OFFICER CASUALTIES DURING THE MONTH OF MARCH, 1919.

2/Lieut. G.H.B.Hodges, proceeded to L. of C. Area No. 47, 4-3-19.
Captain A.G.N.Dixey, M.C. on leave to U.K. retained for Demobilisation.
2/Lieut. T.Garratt, Invalided to U.K. (Sick) 13-3-19.
2/Lieut. W.N.Smith, Left Battn. for Demobilisation, 25.3.19.
Lieut. J.Kilroe,   -do-   -do-   25-3-19.
  do. H.S.Latham,   -do-   -do-   25-3-19.
  do. E.W.Shaw,   -do-   -do-   25-3-19.
Captain G.F.S.Brownlow,) Proceeded to join 1/5th Bn. The BORDER
Lieut. P.Earle.   )   REGIMENT, A/Occupation,
  do. E.Crossley, M.C.)   26-3-19.
2/Lieut. D.Slack.   )
  do. A.Drabble, M.M.)
  do. G.D.Ramsay.   )
  do. A.E.Owen.   )
  do. H.D.Telford.   )
  do. H.Branham, M.C.)
Lieut. P.Darlington, M.C. Left Battn. for Demobilisation, 15-3-19.
  do. E.H.Shackle, M.C.   -do-   -do-   15-3-19.
  do. J.T.Walley, M.C.   -do-   -do-   15-3-19.
2/Lieut. S.R.Pike,   -do-   -do-   15-3-19.
2/Lieut. K.E.Lodge, Proceeded to join 1/5th Bn. The Border Regt,
                    Army of Occupation, 30-3-19.

OTHER RANKS.

  NUMBER OF OTHER RANKS TO U.K. FOR DEMOBILISATION :-   21.
  PROCEEDED TO JOIN 1/5th Bn. The BORDER REGT., 26-3-19. ;- 199.
      -do-   -do-   -do-   30-3-19. :-   1.
  To. UNITED KINGDOM, RE-ENLISTED :- 9.
  TO COLOGNE ON ANIMAL CONDUCTING DUTY 15-3-19, AND RETAINED BY
  2ND ARMY :-
          25.

  SICK EVACUATIONS, MEN DETACHED AND STRUCK OFF STRENGTH, etc.... 21.
  ACCIDENTLY WOUNDED :- 1.

31-3-19.  Lieut. Colonel,
Cdg. 20th Bn. The Manchester Regiment.

SECRET.

Original.

Wd 42 25

WAR DIARY
of
20TH BATTALION THE MANCHESTER REGIMENT.
1st APRIL to 30th APRIL, 1919.
VOLUME. XXXXII

2.5.19.

A C Cowdon Lieut. Colonel,
Cdg. 20th Bn. The Manchester Regt.

20th BATTALION,
THE MANCHESTER
REGIMENT.
No.........................
Date.......................

WAR DIARY
INTELLIGENCE SUMMARY for April 1919 VOLUME 42

Army Form C. 2118.

(Erase heading not required.)

Instructions regarding War Diaries and Intelligence Summaries are contained in F. S. Regs., Part II. and the Staff Manual respectively. Title pages will be prepared in manuscript.

Place	Date	Hour	Summary of Events and Information	Remarks and references to Appendices
CAMBRAI	APRIL 1st		Cadre Strength – Men employed on Regimental Duties	Dk
	2nd		}	
	3rd		Men employed on Regimental Duties	Dk
	4th		}	
	5th			
	6th		Church Parades	Dk
	7th		}	
	8th		Men employed on Regimental Duties Inspection of	
	9th		clothing arms equipment etc.	Dk
	10th		}	
	11th			
	12th			
	13th		Church Parades.	
	14th		Entrained H.Q. house №18 Rue Paul ROBERT.	Dk
	15th		Men employed on Regimental Duties. Inspection of	Dk
	16th		clothing arms etc.	Dk

20th SERVICE BATTALION, MANCHESTER REGIMENT.

WAR DIARY
or
INTELLIGENCE SUMMARY.

(Erase heading not required.)

Army Form C. 2118.

Instructions regarding War Diaries and Intelligence Summaries are contained in F. S. Regs., Part II. and the Staff Manual respectively. Title pages will be prepared in manuscript.

Place	Date	Hour	20th SERVICE BATTALION, MANCHESTER REGIMENT. Summary of Events and Information	Remarks and references to Appendices
CAMBLAI ATTACK				
	17th		Regimental Duties as usual.	A.K.
	18th		GOOD FRIDAY – Church Parade.	D.K.
	19th		Regimental Duties.	D.K.
	20th		Church Parade.	D.K.
	21st			
	22nd		Regimental Duties – Inspection carried out as usual.	A.K.
	23rd		Weather very bad – much rain – roads (?)	
	24th			
	25th			
	26th			
	27th		Church Parade	J.N.
	28th		Regimental Duties – Weather still very bad.	
	29th			J.N.
	30th		Regimental Duties – much rain.	

A.C. Croydon Lieutenant Colonel Commanding
20th. Service Battalion Manchester Regiment

A6945 Wt. W11422/M1160 35,000 12/16 D. D. & L. Forms/C./2118/14.

20th Bn. The Manchester Regiment.

CASUALTIES DURING THE MONTH OF APRIL, 1919.

OFFICERS.

2/Lieut. S.W.CASSON, left Battn. for Demobilisation, 7.4.19.

OTHER RANKS.

Demobilised --- 1.

To Army of Occupation.)
1/5th Bn. The) --- 4.
Border Regt.)

Total --- 5.

AcurpAm Lieut. Colonel,
Cdg. 20th Bn. The Manchester Regiment.

2.5.19.

20th Bn. The Manchester Regiment.

REINFORCEMENTS RECEIVED DURING THE MONTH OF APRIL, 1919.

OFFICERS.

-- NIL --

OTHER RANKS

-- 2 -- From Base Hospital.

_____

[signature] Lieut. Colonel,
Cdg. 20th Bn. The Manchester Regiment.

2.5.19.

20th Bn. The Manchester Regiment.

NOMINAL ROLL OF OFFICERS AS ON 30th APRIL, 1919.

Commanding Officer.
Lieut. Colonel, A.C.Croydon, M.C.,D.C.M. ..;.. With Battalion.
(West Yorks Regt.).
Adjutant.
Captain, G.B.Dempsey, M.C. .... With Battalion.
Asst. Adjutant.
Captain, D.Kitchen, M.C. .... With Battalion.
Quartermaster.
Captain, E.W.Sharpe (Duke of Lancs. Yeomanry).. With Battalion.

Lieut. H.S.Painter, M.C. .... In Hospital.
2/Lieut. L.H.Spencer .... On Leave to U.K.
2/Lieut. J.A.Feeney .... With H.Q. Army Burials,
                                                  MEAULTE.
2/Lieut. R.L.Hardisty .... With Battalion.

2.5.19.

A.Croydon Lieut. Colonel,
Cdg. 20th Bn. The Manchester Regiment.

20 Manchesters

WAR DIARY
or
INTELLIGENCE SUMMARY.
(Erase heading not required.)

Army Form C. 2118.

Of 8 43

Place	Date	Hour	Summary of Events and Information	Remarks and references to Appendices
Cambrai	May 1st 2nd 3rd 4th	—	Battalion at Cadre Strength. Men employed on Regimental duties	DK
	5th 6th 7th 8th 9th 10th 11th		Church Parades	DK
			There is nothing to report. The weather has been particularly fine.	DK
	12th		Church Parade	DK
	13th 14th 15th 16th 17th		Nothing eventful. All the men of the Cadre are employed on Regimental duties. The weather is very fine.	DK
	18th		Church Parade	DK
	19th 20th		Nothing unusual to report. Cadre reduced. The numbers now are 3 Officers and 26 O.R.S.	DK DK DK

Army Form C. 2118.

WAR DIARY
or
INTELLIGENCE SUMMARY.
(Erase heading not required.)

Instructions regarding War Diaries and Intelligence Summaries are contained in F. S. Regs., Part II. and the Staff Manual respectively. Title pages will be prepared in manuscript.

Place	Date	Hour	Summary of Events and Information	Remarks and references to Appendices
Can Ser	MAY 21		Nothing to report. The weather is particularly fine	S/L
	22			S/L
	23			
	24		Church Parade.	
	25			
	26		There is nothing to report. The weather is still	S/L
	27	8	particularly fine. Men had been employed on Regimental	
	28		duties. Nothing eventful has happened.	
	29			
	30			
	31			

WAR DIARY
or
INTELLIGENCE SUMMARY.
(Erase heading not required.)

Army Form C. 2118.

20 November

Place	Date	Hour	Summary of Events and Information	Remarks and references to Appendices
Bamburh	1/11		Church Parades	X.
	2/11 3/11 4/11 5/11 6/11 7/11		Regimental Duties. There is nothing of interest to report.	X.
	8/11 9/11 10/11 11/11 12/11 13/11 14/11		Church Parades Regimental Duties	X. X.
	15/11		Cadre reduced to Equipment Guard Strength 2 officers 12 O.R.s	X.
	16/11 17/11 18/11 19/11 20/11 21/11		There is nothing to report. The Equipment Guard of the 3 units in the Brigade have amalgamated for the purpose of meeting.	X.Y.

Army Form C. 2118.

WAR DIARY
or
INTELLIGENCE SUMMARY.
(Erase heading not required.)

Instructions regarding War Diaries and Intelligence Summaries are contained in F. S. Regs., Part II. and the Staff Manual respectively. Title pages will be prepared in manuscript.

Place	Date	Hour	Summary of Events and Information	Remarks and references to Appendices
CAMBRIN	June 22		Church Parade	Sd/-
	23			Sd/-
	24		Regimental Duties	
	25		nothing to Report	
	26			
	27			
	28			
	29		Church Parade.	Sd/-
	30		nothing to Report	Sd/-

www.ingramcontent.com/pod-product-compliance
Lightning Source LLC
Chambersburg PA
CBHW081554160426
43191CB00011B/1927